Kaleidoscope

the Smart Way

Sharon Sebrow

DEDICATION

To my brother, Joel, of blessed memory.
Your creativity was always an inspiration.

ברוך אתה ה׳ אלקינו מלך העולם שהחינו וקימנו והגיענו לזמן הזה

Blessed are you, G-d, who has kept us in life, has preserved us, and enabled us to reach this occasion.

Located in Paducah, Kentucky, the American Quilter's Society (AQS) is dedicated to promoting the accomplishments of today's quilters. Through its publications and events, AQS strives to honor today's quiltmakers and their work and to inspire future creativity and innovation in quiltmaking.

Text© 2009, Author, Sharon Sebrow
Artwork© 2009, American Quitler's Society

Executive Book Editor: Andi Milam Reynolds
Senior Editor: Linda Baxter Lasco
Graphic Design: Lynda Smith
Cover Design: Michael Buckingham
Photography: Charles R. Lynch

Additional copies of this book may be ordered from the American Quilter's Society, PO Box 3290, Paducah, KY 42002-3290, or online at www.AmericanQuilter.com.

Library of Congress Cataloging-in-Publication Data

Sebrow, Sharon.
  Kaleidoscope the smart way / by Sharon Sebrow.
      p. cm.
  ISBN 978-1-57432-977-3
  1. Patchwork--Patterns. 2. Quilting. 3. Kaleidoscope quilts. I. Title.

  TT835.S4315 2009
  746.46'041--dc22
                                        2008051599

American Quilter's Society
P. O. Box 3290 • Paducah, KY 42002-3290
www.AmericanQuilter.com

Proudly printed and bound in the United States of America

ACKNOWLEDGMENTS

Thank you to my family: my husband, Zvi, who, in lieu of flowers, knew me well enough to bring home a quilt magazine to get out of the doghouse; Devorah, who would sit so quietly at my side giving me time for sewing; Dina, who was always there to check out my new designs and help me sandwich and baste; Yosefa, who picked up needle in hand and took to quilting to keep me company; Hillel, who is always happy to help me arrange my blocks; and Avi, who is always there to give me the honesty only a toddler can offer, adopting as "his" the quilts he likes best. To my family: Thanks. Your love, patience, encouragement, and acceptance of take-out dinners has made it possible for me to reach this milestone. I love you all.

Thank you to my parents, Irene and Marty; my step-parents, Claire and Henry; and my sister, Toby, for recognizing my love for crafting and needlework. Without your support and encouragement of the hobbies of my youth and continued support, I would not be who I am today.

Thank you to Denise Trend, owner of the Cozy Quilt Shoppe in River Edge, New Jersey, for her generosity of time, space, materials, and a bottomless cup of coffee. Thanks to all the ladies at the Cozy Quilt Shoppe for their help, support, and suggestions.

Thank you to my dear friends: Sharon Laufer, who dove into a few cartons of scraps, only to come out with a new career for me; Ellen Greenberg Friedman, for your amazing color sense and for keeping me focused on reaching each goal on my "list"; Marian Kugelmass, for your eagerness to learn quilting and for showing me the left-handed point of view; and Amy Winn-Dworkin, for your friendship and interest in this project as I progressed from prototype to prototype. You have all been a wonderful sisterhood giving your support, time, and advice.

Thank you, Mary Carvajal, my assistant. You have been there for me as a sounding board, a design consultant, and especially a friend.

Thank you to American Quilter's Society and its entire staff, particularly Barbara Smith, Andi Reynolds, and Linda Baxter Lasco for their support, advice, and enthusiasm for my project. I have learned so much from you, yet I know I have so much more to learn.

CONTENTS

INTRODUCTION TO A NEW CONCEPT

The traditional way of making the Kaleidoscope block begins with the cutting of 8 narrow triangles and sewing them together into an octagon, matching the center intersection of the 8 sharp triangle points. To complete the block, 4 more triangles must be cut and added to the corners to make the block square. That seems simple enough, except when the sewing machine eats the beginning of the seam, or when the points separate at the end of the seam.

The difficulties in sewing lead to difficulties in getting the center points to match. Therefore, the block is considered somewhat challenging and, because of the frustration factor, not recommended for beginning quilters.

As a quilting teacher, I have always tried to inspire beginning quilters to try blocks that seem "out of their league" by offering quick and simple ways to achieve the look of a block with methods such as strip-piecing and faux triangles. I often teach these methods to my beginner students with great success.

I have long admired the traditional Kaleidoscope and its versatility when combined with other blocks and thought it would be a great block to inspire beginning quilters.

I realized that the Kaleidoscope's center intersecting points of 45 degrees for each triangle were the same as the basic Pinwheel block, with just a slight rotation. So I set my goal to find a simple way to cut the outer edges of a pinwheel to create the center octagon shape of the Kaleidoscope block.

I also noticed that not all the Kaleidoscope blocks had a different fabric in the corners. Some had cor-

ner pieces that could be kite-shaped, eliminating the need for piecing a triangle at the corner.

I developed the Kaleidoscope Smart-Plate® template to aid in assembling both types of Kaleidoscope blocks—the 8-patch version with kite-shaped wedges in the corners and the 12-patch version with 8 wedges creating a center octagon and separate triangles pieced in the corners to square the block.

The template comes in two sizes. You can make finished blocks from 2" to 6" with the smaller template and from 2" to 12" with the larger template. Simply start with the basic Pinwheel block. Then use the Kaleidoscope Smart-Plate to cut the version and size of the Kaleidoscope block you want.

You can trace the Smart-Plate template pattern on page 92 onto template plastic to make the projects in this book. See for yourself how versatile the traditional Kaleidoscope block is by using it in a variety of settings—side-by-side, with alternating blocks, in sashings, in borders, and with fabric scraps.

Make a quilt from the book or make your own design. Whether you are trying this block for the first time or are looking for a fast project with a WOW factor, prepare to be amazed by how easily and quickly it can be done when you make a Kaleidoscope the Smart Way.

HOW TO USE THIS BOOK

This book is designed to teach you a brand-new technique using a brand-new template. Similar to strip piecing, patches are sewn and then cut across the seams to reveal the desired block, so this technique is not recommended for hand piecing.

The patterns in this book call for 6" finished Kaleidoscope blocks. A pattern for the Smart-Plate template is provided on page 92. Make your own template by tracing the shape and markings on template plastic. A clear, laser-cut and printed acrylic Kaleidoscope Smart-Plate template is also available (see Resources, page 94).

Because the basis of the technique is the pinwheel, I offer a number of different methods to make half-square triangle units and tips to get perfect centers. See The Pinwheel Block beginning on page 9.

You will not find instructions on sandwiching, basting, or quilting as there are many wonderful books on those subjects. For instructions and tips on borders and bindings, refer to Tips for Borders and Binding (pages 19–21).

Following the Patterns

All of the patterns note which version(s) of the Kaleidoscope blocks are used and suggest which half-square triangle method to use. A key illustrates the half-square triangle combinations, rectangles, and squares needed for the blocks in the pattern.

Patterns are rated for difficulty with one symbol for smart, two for clever, and three for brilliant.

The patterns illustrate each of the Pinwheel combinations needed, how they should be trimmed to make the Kaleidoscope blocks for the sample quilt, and a complete quilt top diagram. For tips and ideas to help make these quilts even easier, I have included "Sharon's Shortcuts" in boxed-off areas in the patterns section, offering suggestions on getting past problem spots.

Basic Tools

Basic tools for machine quilting are, just that—basic. These are the "must-haves" whether you are working on a Kaleidoscope quilt, Nine Patch, or any other pattern. However, many tools can be considered more of a category, with a number of options available. For instance, a quilting ruler can come in a variety of sizes and shapes. So which is the size or shape best for your needs? A list of basic machine piecing tools follows with my suggestions for what would be the best to have in your quilting toolbox.

Rotary Cutter

The rotary cutter comes in a variety of sizes and handle options, each with a unique way of exposing the blade. I consider safety to be the biggest issue with the rotary cutter and recommend the styles with an automatic blade closure like the type that exposes the blade only when the handle is compressed, although it may not be the best for a quilter with arthritic hands or other hand issues.

The 45mm is a great all-purpose blade size. The 60mm is great for cutting through more than 6 layers of fabric. The 20mm and smaller is more appropriate for cutting around curved templates.

Don't forget to change your blade. If you find the blade is not cutting as well as it used to or if it is skipping sections, the cause is probably a dull or nicked blade.

Cutting Mat

My advice is to get the largest mat you can afford and to store it properly. The larger mats allow you to cut fabric without doubling the fold. This will help to cut your strips straight. Be sure to keep the mat stored flat and away from heat to keep it in perfect cutting shape. Many quilters like to have a Lazy Susan-style cutting mat that can be rotated to avoid moving the fabric mid-cut. For our purposes, this can be useful but it's not necessary.

The Kaleidoscope Smart-Plate® Template

My Smart-Plate is the basis of the cutting techniques outlined in this book (see Resources, page 94). Instructions for the using the Kaleidoscope Smart-Plate and all its markings are included in this book (pages 14–18). Additionally, it has the necessary markings to change the size of the finished block from 6" down to 2". On page 92 you will find a printed template that can be used to make all of the 6" finished Kaleidoscope blocks in the sample quilts included in the pattern section. If you copy it onto transparent template plastic, you will be able to see your seam lines.

Rulers

There are two basic ruler shapes I advise any quilter to own—the long rectangle and square.

WEB OF TROUBLE variation (page 64)

The long rectangle: 6½" x 24" to 8½" x 24½"

The length of this ruler is helpful because it will extend across a half-width of fabric, making it easier to cut strips. This ruler can also be used for marking quilting lines and is instrumental in squaring up your quilts to prepare for finishing.

The square rulers: 6½" and 12½"

Why both? The larger square ruler is used for cutting the large squares used in making half-square triangles. It can cut large or small squares. Working with the smaller ruler is less cumbersome when cutting smaller squares and squaring up smaller patches.

A Working Sewing Machine

This may seem unnecessary to mention, but regular machine prep and maintenance are the keys to keeping your machine at the top of its game. Check your machine when starting a new project. Thread tensions need to be set properly for the fabric of the project you are working on. Often one can change settings while working on something "special" and then forget to change them back.

A new needle can save you time and frustration trying to figure out why you have skipped stitches or frayed and broken threads. Take the time to clean the lint from the bobbin case and under the throat plate. This will help keep your machine running smoothly as well. Get into the habit of doing these things before starting each new project.

Pressing Surface and Iron with Automatic Shut-off

Because you are cutting, sewing, pressing, cutting, sewing, pressing, etc., you don't want to have to turn your iron on and wait for it to warm up each time you get up to press something. But chances are you may get distracted doing a particular task that takes longer than expected and forget to turn it off before leaving your work area. An iron with an automatic shut-off is worth the investment. It is convenient and safer!

A note on pressing: When pressing with steam, be sure to give the fabric a moment to cool down. The steam will dampen the fabric. If you pick it up while it is hot and damp, the fabric can become distorted. Because our Kaleidoscope blocks are cut with exposed bias, you must be careful not to pull at your fabrics when pressing. Try not to move the iron around too much and if you feel you must, do so with a "light hand" and move in the direction of the grain of the fabric.

Preparing Your Fabrics

If you prewash your fabric, do not use fabric softener in the washer or the dryer. The sizing used by the manufacturer is removed with washing, making the fabric soft and supple—not the optimal state for machine piecing. Use a stabilizing medium, such as spray-starch or sizing, and the fabric and bias edges will hold their shape better.

THE PINWHEEL BLOCK

Half-Square Triangle (HST) Units

Starting with accurate half-square triangle units makes the matching of the triangle points in the center of the block a much easier task.

There are a number of ways to make half-square triangles. These can range from the most basic method of sewing two triangles into a square to using a printed triangle paper roll. You can make your half-square triangles whichever way you like best.

I find that the three methods presented here, along with a faux triangle method, work well. They are quick "sew-and-cut" methods. Depending on the type of quilt you're making, one method may work better for you than another.

HST Method #1 produces 2 half-square triangles with the same color combinations. It's a great method for scrappy quilt designs. This method is convenient when using precut 5" squares and fabric scraps.

HST Method #2 produces 8 half-square triangles with the same color combinations—great for more organized scrappy designs when the same fabrics are used within a block. This method is convenient when using fat eighths or fat quarters.

HST Method #3, which I have found to be the quickest method, produces multiple half-square triangles with the same color combinations. This is great for quilts that are made with only a few fabrics throughout the quilt.

The faux triangle method can be used in sashing and border sections as well as in other patterns to avoid unnecessary piecing.

For each finished Kaleidoscope block size, the sizes for the pinwheels, half-square triangles, squares, and strips needed for the various meth-ods of making half-square triangles are included in the table on page 13.

Sewing Half-Square Triangles— 3 Methods

HST Method #1

This method uses small squares and produces 2 identical half-square triangles. They can be used in different blocks for a super scrappy look or to-gether in the same block for a more unified block.

Layer 2 squares right sides together. Draw a di-agonal line from one corner to the opposite corner on the top square. Sew ¼" from each side of the drawn line. Cut along the line to separate the 2 half-square triangles. Press open with the seam allowance toward the darker fabric.

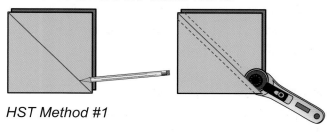

HST Method #1

HST Method #2

This method uses larger squares and produces 8 identical half-square triangles—enough to make two Pinwheel blocks. They can be used separately in different blocks or together in the same block for a unified look.

Layer 2 squares right sides together. Draw 2 diag-onal lines from each corner to the opposite corner, marking an X on the top square, and lines verti-cally and horizontally through the middle as shown (a, page 10).

Sew ¼" from each side of the diagonal lines, *not* the vertical or horizontal (b). Cut on all the drawn lines to separate the 8 half-square triangles (c & d). If you find your squares seem to be puckered when the diagonal sewing is done, press the sewn squares flat before cutting apart.

Press open with the seam allowance toward the darker fabric.

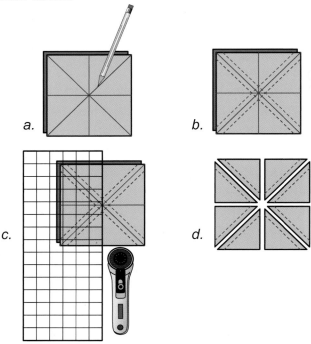

a.

b.

c.

d.

HST Method #2

Troubleshooting Methods #1 & #2

If you find your completed half-square triangles are coming out just slightly smaller than the desired size, don't despair. This is very common and is caused by a too generous seam allowance or by slightly inaccurate cutting. A simple solution is to begin with a slightly larger square and then trim the half-square triangles down to the precise desired size.

If you are using Method #1, add ⅛" to the size of the squares you begin with. If you are using Method #2, add ¼" to the starting square. Follow the trimming instructions on page 11 to trim the half-square triangles to the perfect size.

HST Method #3

For multiple HST units in the same fabric combinations, cut strips the full width of the fabrics, selvage to selvage. With right sides together, sew along both long edges of the strips with a ¼" seam allowance, creating a long tube.

Place the corner of a square ruler along the tube as shown, aligning the stitching line with the unfinished HST size measurement on both sides of the square ruler (as noted by arrows).

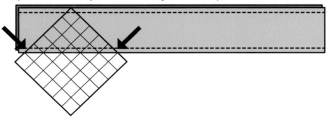

Using a rotary cutter, cut along the corner of the ruler for your first half-square triangle.

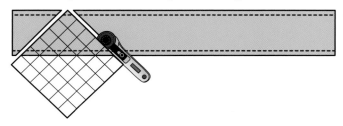

Place the ruler on the tube aligning the same measurement with the opposite seam and one edge of the ruler with the cut edge of the tube. Be sure to align the seam with the appropriate measurement on both sides of the square ruler. Cut along the side of the ruler for the second half-square triangle.

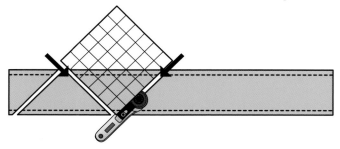

Continue to work this way to the end of the sewn strip tube.

Press the HST units open with the seam allowance toward the darker fabric. The stitches at the point should pop open. If they do not, simply remove the stitches with a seam ripper.

Trimming Half-Square Triangles

Step 1. Lay your HST unit face-up on a rotary cutting mat with the diagonal seam running from the top right corner to the bottom left corner. Place your square ruler with the 45-degree line on the seam with some excess fabric peeking out along the top and the right side of the ruler. Adjust your ruler so the desired measurement on the ruler is completely filled with the half-square triangle beneath (a). If it is not filled completely, the half-square triangle will be too small.

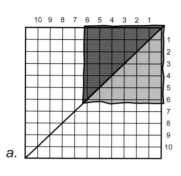

a.

Step 2. Using the ruler as a guide, cut off the excess along the top and right side of the ruler with your rotary cutter (b).

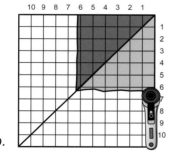

b.

Step 3. Rotate the half-square triangle 180 degrees so the 45-degree line on the ruler is once again on the seam and the newly trimmed edges are along the desired measurement markings on the ruler. There should be some excess peeking out of the top and right side of the ruler (c).

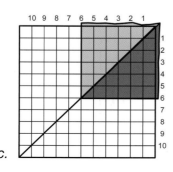

c.

Step 4. Using the ruler as a guide, cut off the excess along the top and side of the ruler with your rotary cutter (d).

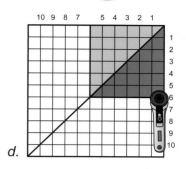

d.

Simplified Pinwheel Block Construction and Faux Half-Square Triangles

There are times when you will only need one or two half-square triangles for a pattern block, such as those used in pieced borders and frames. (For examples of this, see the borders of the sample quilt patterns HANAMACHI, SQUARE IN A STAR, and APPLE BLOSSOM.)

In these cases you do not need to piece an entire Pinwheel. You can choose to use solid rectangles or squares to make up the parts of the block adjacent to each other that use the same fabric.

Cut a plain square the same size as the half-square triangle it replaces. For instance, the 6" finished Kaleidoscope block begins with (4) 4½" half-square triangles. Therefore, a square replacing any of these HSTs should be 4½" x 4½".

Cut a plain rectangle the same size as 2 half-square triangles sewn together. For instance, in the same 6" finished Kaleidoscope block, two 4½" half-square triangles sewn together would be 4½" x 8½". Therefore, a rectangle replacing any pair of these half-square triangles should be 4½" x 8½".

Instead of a plain square and a HST combination, you can use a faux half-square triangle technique. Cut a square the same size as the half-square triangle it's replacing. Align it with one end of an appropriately-sized rectangle and stitch across the diagonal, corner to corner, being sure to sew it in the correct direction to place the faux half-square triangle in the correct location on the block.

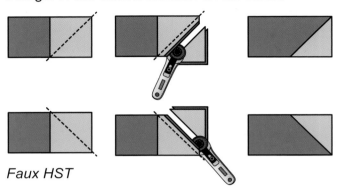

Faux HST

Eliminate some bulk by trimming the excess layers of the square and the rectangle, leaving a ¼" seam allowance. Press open with the seam allowance toward the darker fabric.

Sewing the Pinwheel Block

Once the half-square triangles are made, you can sew them into pairs, then sew the pairs into Pinwheel blocks. Take care when positioning the half-square triangles. The orientation of the HSTs is the same in both halves of the pinwheel. Then one half is rotated and the halves are sewn together. Press seam in the same direction as the HST seams.

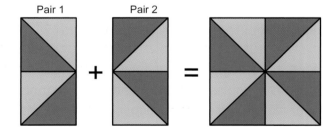

Matching Center Seams Without Losing Points

Press each pair of half-square triangles the same way so when you turn one pair for sewing the final seam, the "bumps" created by the seam allowances will be pressed in opposite directions. Nestle the bumps against each other.

There are three of these bumps to nestle—the first diagonal seam (a), the seam between the half-square

triangles (b), and the second diagonal seam (c). Be sure that all three are nestled at the same time.

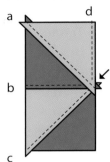

When sewing the seam (d), aim for the intersection of the three previously sewn seams (designated by the arrow). It is at this intersection that the points are either made or lost in the block. In a perfect world, this intersection of seams should be ¼" from the raw edges you are sewing.

Basting a Partial Seam

Make life easier—to avoid removing a full seam, start by using a long machine basting stitch at the intersection area only. Begin sewing ½" or so from the intersection and sew for approximately one inch. Then check the points from the right side. If you are unhappy, you are only "unsewing" about one inch of basting. When you are satisfied with the points, change your stitch length back to a regular stitch and sew the full seam, sewing directly over the basting stitches.

Press each end of the final seam in opposite directions so the seams in the block are all pressed either clockwise or counterclockwise, opening what looks like a mini pinwheel at the block's center. The stitches in the seam allowance at the center should pop open (as noted in the illustration). However, if they do not, remove these stitches so the final seam can be separated at the center and pressed flat.

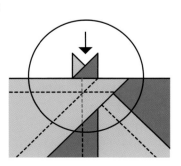

Troubleshooting the Pinwheel Block

Problem: If you find that your center points are not satisfactory, here are some tips to help you get them where you want them.

Solution: Check the original seams in your half-square triangles. If the seam between the first two is off, the centers will never line up.

Check the seam allowances at the intersecting points. The seam allowance from the raw edge (the arrow in the figure on page 12) should be ¼" from the intersection of the a, b, and c seams.

If you find that one is too large, trim the raw edge so it is ¼" from the intersection.

If you find that one is too small, either note the difference and adjust your alignment to make up the difference or remove the incorrect seam and resew.

Pinwheel Sizes

Because the Pinwheel blocks are a base block to be trimmed down to make the Kaleidoscope blocks, as long as the Pinwheel is at least as large as or larger than necessary, the Kaleidoscope blocks will be easily cut to the desired size. For this reason, the sizes given below may have been rounded-up for ease of measuring and cutting.

Using the Cutting Sizes Table

All of the patterns use 6" finished Kaleidoscope blocks. If you'd like to make smaller blocks, find the finished measurement of the desired Kaleidoscope block version (8-patch or 12-patch) on the table below. Follow the row across to establish the Pinwheel size and the size of the half-square triangles that will make the unfinished size Pinwheel block you need. Then choose the half-square triangle method for the size squares or strips you need to construct them.

Table: Cutting Sizes

FINISHED BLOCK SIZE	PINWHEEL BLOCK SIZE (UNFINISHED)	HST SIZE UNFINISHED)	METHOD #1	METHOD #2	METHOD #3
8-Patch Kaleidoscope			Cut square	Cut square	Cut strip width
6"	8½"	4½"	4⅞"	9¾"	3½" (9)*
5"	7¼"	3⅞"	4¼"	8½"	3" (11)*
4"	6"	3¼"	3⅝"	7¼"	2⅝" (13)*
3"	4¾"	2⅝"	3"	6"	2⅛" (17)*
2"	3½"	2"	2⅜"	4¾"	1¾" (21)*
12-Patch Kaleidoscope	**Pinwheel Block Size (unfinished)**	HST Size	Cut square	Cut square	Cut strip width
6"	7"	3¾"	4⅛"	8¼"	3" (11)*
5"	6"	3¼"	3⅝"	7¼"	2⅝" (13)*
4"	5"	2¾"	3⅛"	6¼"	2¼" (15)*
3"	4"	2¼"	2⅝"	5¼"	1⅞" (19)*
2"	3"	1¾"	2⅛"	4¼"	1½" (25)*

* number of HSTs from one strip

TRIMMING THE 8-PATCH KALEIDOSCOPE BLOCK RIGHT-HANDED

Align the template's wedge-shaped lines with your pinwheel seams with the long straight edge on your right. Cut along the long straight edge as shown (a).

Rotate the block clockwise 90 degrees, align the template as before, and cut along the long straight edge (b).

Repeat two more times as shown (c & d).

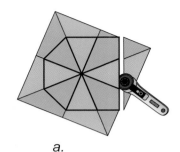
a.

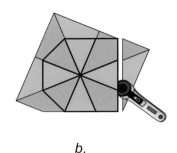
b.

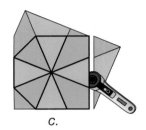
c.

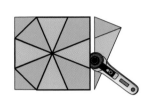
d.

TRIMMING THE 8-PATCH KALEIDOSCOPE BLOCK LEFT-HANDED

Align the template's wedge-shaped lines with your pinwheel seams with the long straight edge on your left. Cut along the long straight edge as shown (a).

Rotate the block counter-clockwise 90 degrees, align the template as before, and cut along the long straight edge (b).

Repeat two more times as shown (c & d).

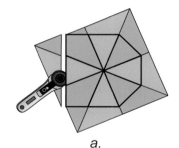
a.

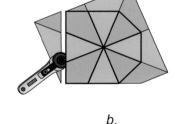
b.

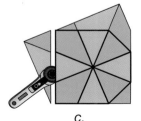
c.

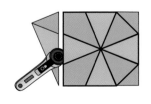
d.

TRIMMING THE 12-PATCH KALEIDOSCOPE BLOCK RIGHT-HANDED

Align the template's wedge-shaped lines with your pinwheel seams with the long straight edge toward you (a).

Make 4 cuts along the right side and the 3 short edges as shown (b).

Rotate the block 180 degrees, aligning the template with the pinwheel seams as before (c).

Make 4 cuts along the right side and the 3 short edges as shown (d).

Cut 2 squares in half on the diagonal (e). (See the Pieced Corner Sizes table, page 17, for the size.)

Sew the triangles to the corner wedges (f).

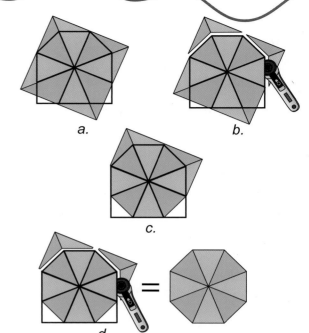

TRIMMING THE 12-PATCH KALEIDOSCOPE BLOCK LEFT-HANDED

Align the template's wedge-shaped lines with your pinwheel seams with the long straight edge toward you (a).

Make 4 cuts along the left side and the 3 short edges as shown (b).

Rotate the block 180 degrees, aligning the template with the pinwheel seams as before (c).

Make 4 cuts along the left side and the 3 short edges as shown (d).

Cut 2 squares in half on the diagonal (e). (See the Pieced Corner Sizes table, page 17, for the size.)

Sew the triangles to the corner wedges (f).

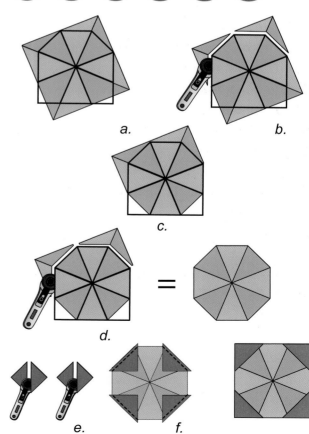

USING THE KALEIDOSCOPE SMART-PLATE®

The 6½" Kaleidoscope Smart-Plate® template is designed with guidelines to make the more commonly used 6" finished block size. However, it is also marked with additional guidelines so you can make smaller blocks, from 2" to 5". Note that the markings on the ruler are the FINISHED block size. Your cut block will measure ½" larger to allow for the seam allowance.

A larger 12½" template is available, designed with guidelines to make blocks from 2" to 12".

Smaller 8-Patch Blocks—2" and up

Refer to the Cutting Sizes table (page 13) for the correct patch and Pinwheel block sizes needed for the size block you wish to make.

Place the kite-shaped V of the desired finished block size on the seams of the wedge to be the block corner. The point of the V should align with the intersection of the seams in the center of the pinwheel. Cut along the long side of the Smart-Plate to trim one side of the corner. (Illustration is for right-handed quilters; for left-handed quilters, use the other set of kite-shaped Vs so the Smart-Plate's long side will be on your left.)

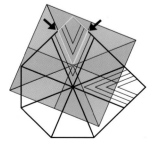 

Rotate the block ¼ way around, realigning the same V with the next corner wedge of the pinwheel.

Again, use the long edge of the Smart-Plate to cut against, and complete trimming the remaining two corners of the block in the desired size this way. (When working on a block small enough, you can use adjacent sides of the template around the kite-shaped section to make two cuts with one placement. Turn the block halfway around to trim the remaining two sides with the placement of the kite shape on the opposite corner wedge.

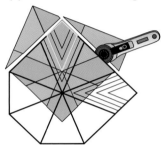

Smaller 12-Patch Blocks with Pieced Corners—2" and up

Start with a Pinwheel block or an already-trimmed 8-patch Kaleidoscope block.

On the Corner Cut section of the template there are two adjacent wedges of guidelines. Choose the appropriately sized Vs and align them with the seams of the pinwheel or corner wedge to be trimmed.

In the illustration, the desired size is a 4" finished block. Therefore, the 4" Block guidelines are aligned with the seams on the pinwheel (indicated with yellow) and the points of the Vs are aligned with the intersection of the seams in the center of the pinwheel (noted with a red dot). The red arrows show where the edge of the Kaleidoscope Smart-Plate meets the edges of the pinwheel.

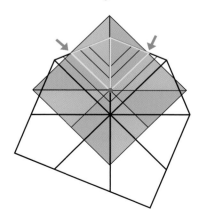

Use a rotary cutter to trim away the excess fabric between the two red arrows (in the figure on page 16). Rotate the block 90 degrees and repeat for the next set of wedges. Repeat two more times, until all 8 wedges are trimmed and an octagon kaleidoscope is achieved.

Preparing Corner Triangles

Once the central octagon shape is complete, triangles must be pieced to four alternating wedges to make the block square. Determine which wedges will be in the corner positions. Use the Pieced Corner Sizes table on this page to determine the size squares to cut into triangles for the corners.

For each block, cut 2 squares the appropriate size. Cut each square once on the diagonal to produce 4 triangles. To position the triangles, find the center of a corner wedge by folding the wedge in half, aligning its 2 side seams. Mark the fold with a pin or a crease. Fold a triangle in half and mark the center of the long side. Align the center marks, right sides together, and pin in place. Join the triangle to the wedge with a ¼" seam allowance.

Combination Blocks

Combination blocks are blocks that have some pieced corners and some not pieced. This allows for wonderful design options that can change the overall look of the quilt without having to piece corners with the same fabric that was cut away. This will save you work and time.

Certainly, with time and experience with the template, you will become adept at handling your block and template to be able to predict what should and should not be cut away in a single positioning of the template. While you are still learning, it is suggested you prepare the block in two steps:

Step 1 - Make the basic 8-patch version of the block.

Step 2 - Cut away any corners necessary for your block or use a faux triangle technique for the corners.

To make pieced corner triangles with a faux triangle technique: Cut the appropriately sized square; place it right sides together on the corner of an uncut corner wedge; sew on the diagonal, corner to corner; and fold out the corner triangle. See the table for the appropriate size square as determined by the finished Kaleidoscope block size.

Table: Pieced Corner Sizes

FINISHED BLOCK SIZE	SQUARE CUT ON DIAGONAL	FAUX TRIANGLE SQUARE SIZE
6"	2⅝"	2¼"
5"	2⅜"	2"
4"	2"	1⅝"
3"	1¾"	1⅜"
2"	1½"	1⅛"

Troubleshooting Trimming Problems

Problem: Your pinwheel is too small and the corners of the template stick out over the edge of the block.

Solution: Occasionally, you might find that your base Pinwheel block is too small. You have 3 choices:

Choice 1. If the discrepancy is very small, you can continue to trim as you would otherwise and accept that the seam allowance in the corner will be slightly short. This is not a problem providing that the difference is less than ¼".

Choice 2. Check all seam allowances and original cutting measurements to be sure that all are correct, unsew what needs to be adjusted, and remake the base Pinwheel block.

Choice 3. As you continue to make more pinwheels for additional blocks, make them slightly larger to allow extra for trimming.

Problem: The guidelines on the ruler or the template points do not perfectly line up with the seam lines.

Solution: This can be due to poor pressing or inaccurate sewing of the base pinwheel.

Sometimes a slight stretch or repressing of the pinwheel is all that is needed to make everything line up. If this doesn't help, check the center seams and wedge measurements to make sure that the center of the pinwheel is actually in the center, not slightly off-center, and that the seams meet at the center.

Problem: You trimmed the wrong corner of your 8-patch block.

Solution: When trimming an 8-patch block, if you don't make sure that the corner kite-shaped wedge of the template is situated on the wedge of the pinwheel that is meant to be kite-shaped, you may accidentally cut away the corner.

Instead of "scrapping" the entire block, remove the accidentally-trimmed HST unit, replace it, and then trim properly.

TIPS FOR BORDERS AND BINDING

Borders are an important structural element in these Kaleidoscope quilts. As mentioned earlier, the Kaleidoscope block edges are exposed bias. If they are not held in check by "on grain" borders, they can stretch and distort during the finishing process, resulting in a quilt that may not be square or lie flat. Here are some tips for borders:

• **Measure your quilt top and cut borders to match** – Although patterns give exact cutting measurements for border strips, these measurements are mathematically figured out according to the exact mathematical size the blocks should be. Due to slight inconsistencies from one quilter to another, these measurements may not be the actual size of your quilt top. Therefore, it is extremely important to measure your quilt top before cutting the border strips.

Many beginning quilters will cut border strips longer than the size that is needed, figuring to sew from one end and cut away any excess at the other end. This will lead to a border that doesn't lie flat and a quilt that isn't squared at the corners.

The quilt will need to be "squared-off," which involves trimming away from borders or blocks creating a square-cornered quilt with borders that taper off at the sides or blocks that are cut off at the corners.

I know conventional wisdom says to measure through the center of the quilt top for the length of the border strips and to ease in any extra fullness as the borders are sewn. The reason for this is that the sides will most likely NOT be the right or the same measurement. However, the center measurement can vary in size from the actual quilt side measurements by quite a lot.

Try the following method for determining border strip lengths:

Measure the opposite sides of the quilt top. If the measurements between two opposite sides are off by an inch or so, take a good look at the seams along the edges; any seams that are frayed or opening should be resewn and/or reinforced. If the measurements are still off, look between the blocks, to see if any seams can be "taken in" or "let out." Remember, even a few threads' difference between a few seams can quickly add up to ½" or more. Try to even the sides out as much as possible. Then cut the border strips the same length.

• **Cut the border strips extra wide** – When quilts are machine quilted, often they are stretched and skewed. Choose to cut the outer border strips slightly wider than the pattern calls for to allow for trimming after quilting is complete. This will ensure a square and even edge to bind.

• **Match the fabric print or stripes on pieced border strips** – When you have to piece border strips that have a noticeable printed pattern, it is wise to try to match the print to make the seam less noticeable.

Find the repeat of the fabric's print and cut 2 (or more, if necessary) strips from the same segment of the repeat.

Place one strip horizontally, right side up on your work surface. Fold under and press the right-hand end of the strip on a 45-degree angle.

Place the second strip horizontally right side up on your work surface. Lay the folded section of the first strip over the left-hand end of the second strip, matching the print on the strips. Place a dab of fabric glue stick on the folded-under portion of the strip to hold the strips in place.

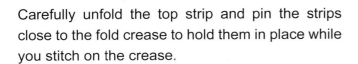

Carefully unfold the top strip and pin the strips close to the fold crease to hold them in place while you stitch on the crease.

Trim the excess, leaving ¼" seam allowance. When the strips are opened, the seam should create an unbroken motif.

Folded Borders

Inserting a folded border is probably the simplest way to add dimensional detail to a quilt.

Cut a strip of contrasting fabric approximately 1"–1½" wide by the necessary length. Fold in half lengthwise, press, and sandwich the folded strip between the edge of the quilt top and the border you are adding, aligning all the raw edges.

To miter the flange strips at the corners, fold at a 45-degree angle when pinning the folded border into place. Sew through all thicknesses with a ¼" seam allowance. The result will be a narrow flange that frames the quilt top and separates it from the border.

Depending on which way you would like the flange to fall, press the seam allowance in the opposite direction. (That is, if you want the flange to lie along the quilt blocks, press seam allowances toward the border. If you want it to lie along the borders, press the seam allowances toward the quilt blocks.)

Mitered Borders

Mitering a border can give the effect of a picture frame when used with a printed motif stripe (border print). It is simple to do, but takes a little extra effort. With the right fabric and the right quilt, the effort pays off.

Cut your four border strips to fit the actual edge of the quilt top, plus 2 times the width of the border (or multiple borders), plus 2 inches.

In our example the quilt top measures 47". We are using a finished 1", 2" and a 2½" for our inner, middle, and outer borders. Together they will add up to 5½" plus ½" for seam allowance, a total of 6". This is multiplied by 2 to allow for the width of the border on opposite sides of the quilt top. The extra 2" allows for a margin for error and the seam allowances (47 + 12 + 2 = 61").

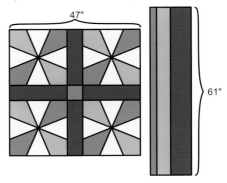

Sew the 3 border strips together for all 4 sides. Press the seam allowances on 2 borders in one direction (toward the inner border) and 2 in the other direction (toward the outer border.)

Mark, on the wrong side, the center points of the borders and the quilt top sides, top and bottom. You can easily find the center points by folding the strips and quilt top in half and marking at the fold lines.

On the wrong side of the quilt top, mark ¼" from the 4 corners. This will be your start and stop points when sewing. Leaving the ¼" edge unsewn will allow for the Y seam in the mitered corner.

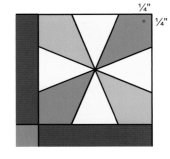

Pin the border strips to the quilt top sides with right sides together. Start by matching the marked center points on the borders and sides and add pins until you get to the corners. This will ensure that your border will be centered. Use the borders pressed in the same direction on opposite sides of the quilt top and the other borders on the remaining sides. The seams will nestle against each other, making it easier to align the corners for a perfect match in the miter.

Start sewing at the ¼" mark from one corner and stop at the ¼" mark from the next corner, reinforcing the stitching at the beginning and the end. Sew all four borders on this way, making sure not to sew past the ¼" mark.

Fold the quilt top from a corner on a 45-degree angle. The borders on either side of this corner should lie one on top of the other with the unsewn excess extending past the fold. Align the seam allowances of the border strips and pin together so they don't shift.

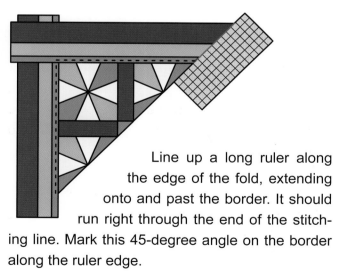

Line up a long ruler along the edge of the fold, extending onto and past the border. It should run right through the end of the stitching line. Mark this 45-degree angle on the border along the ruler edge.

Starting at the point where the border/quilt top seam ends, sew on the marked 45-degree line across the borders. Trim away the excess border fabrics to ¼" seam allowance.

Binding Tips

Among the many questions that I am asked regarding finishing a quilt are these:

How wide do I cut my binding strips? 2¼"

Do I attach binding to the front or back of the quilt first? The front.

Do I use a bias-cut or grain-wise cut strips? Grain-wise, except when I am working with curved edges or striped binding fabric.

Do I attach the strips with a straight or diagonal seam? It depends on my mood!

How do I miter the binding at the corner? This one's worth some details:

Sew up to ¼" from the corner's edge.

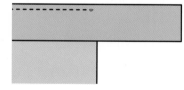

Fold the binding up and away from the quilt top, forming a 45-degree diagonal angle with the unsewn binding off the edge of the quilt as shown.

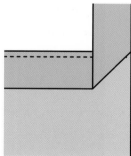

Fold the binding back over itself so the fold you have just made is in line with the raw edge of the quilt along both sides. Begin stitching the next side of the binding ¼" from the corner.

LUCKY STARS

52" x 52 finished size

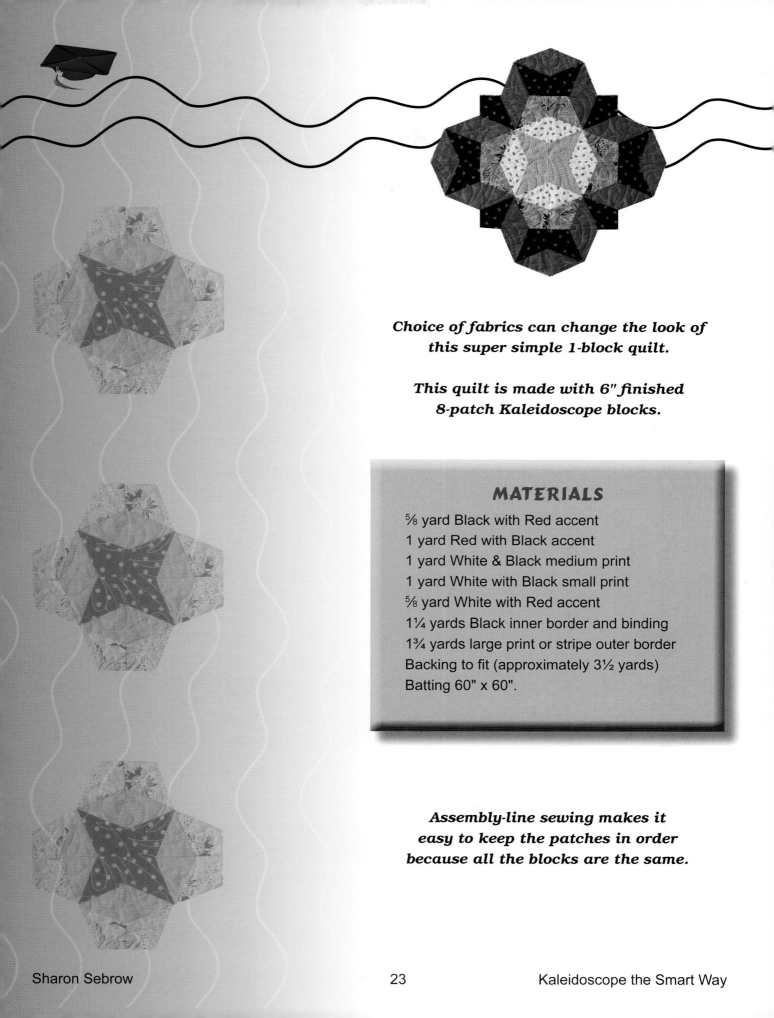

Choice of fabrics can change the look of this super simple 1-block quilt.

This quilt is made with 6" finished 8-patch Kaleidoscope blocks.

MATERIALS

⅝ yard Black with Red accent
1 yard Red with Black accent
1 yard White & Black medium print
1 yard White with Black small print
⅝ yard White with Red accent
1¼ yards Black inner border and binding
1¾ yards large print or stripe outer border
Backing to fit (approximately 3½ yards)
Batting 60" x 60".

Assembly-line sewing makes it easy to keep the patches in order because all the blocks are the same.

MAKING THE PINWHEELS

Use half-square triangle method #2 or #3 (pages 9–11) to make the HST units.

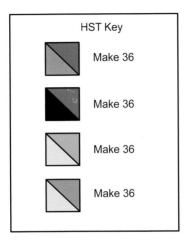

HST Key

Make 36

Make 36

Make 36

Make 36

All the Pinwheel blocks are the same. Follow the diagram to arrange the half-square triangle combinations for the 36 blocks used in this quilt.

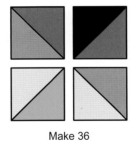

Make 36

SHARON'S SHORTCUT

Sew all the same HST units together at one time to avoid sewing them the wrong way. You will know when something is turned the wrong way immediately because it will not look like all the others.

Use the Kaleidoscope Smart-Plate template to trim the pinwheels into 8-patch Kaleidoscope blocks, starting with the black in the corner wedge position. (See page 14 for detailed cutting instructions.)

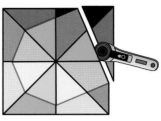

First cut

Make 36

PUTTING THE QUILT TOP TOGETHER

Follow the quilt top assembly diagram (page 25) to arrange the blocks in the overall pattern.

Sew the blocks into rows, then sew the rows together.

BORDERS

Cut 2 strips 2" x 36½" of black inner border fabric and add to opposite sides of the quilt top.

Cut 2 strips 2" x 40½" of black inner border fabric and add to the remaining sides of the quilt top.

Cut 4 strips 7" x 56" from the large print or stripe outer border fabric. Add to all sides of the quilt top and miter the corners. Refer to the directions on page 20–21.

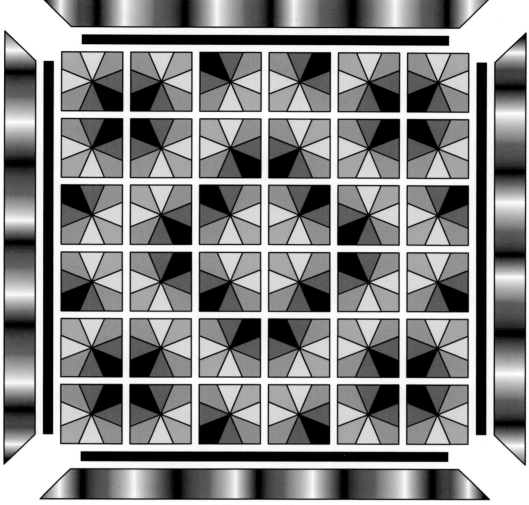

Quilt top assembly

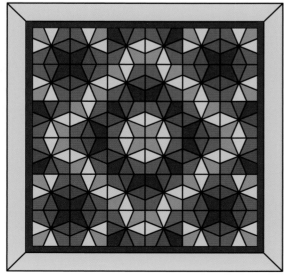 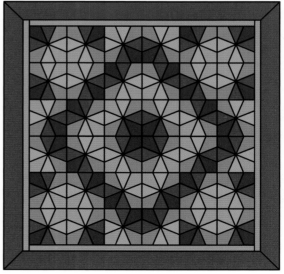

Alternate color ideas

HANAMACHI

70" x 70" finished size

Delicate Kaleidoscope rounds frame
uncommonly shaped stars
with fussy-cut motifs.

This quilt is made with 6" finished
8-patch Kaleidoscope blocks.

MATERIALS

⅞ yard Teal
1⅓ yards Pink
(16) 6½" fussy-cut squares*
3 yards Cream background
2⅛ yards large print Teal Floral for outer border
Backing to fit (approximately 4⅔ yards)
Batting 78" x 78"
⅝ yard Pink binding fabric

*This pattern can be simplified
by eliminating the fussy-cut center.
Either use the same background
fabric in place of the fussy cuts or let
the stars shine by using lighter fabrics
for the stars and one dark color for the
Kaleidoscope rounds as the background.

MAKING THE PINWHEELS

Use half-square triangle method #2 or #3 (pages 9–11) to make the HST units.

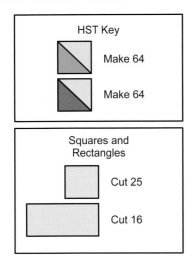

HST Key

Make 64

Make 64

Squares and Rectangles

Cut 25

Cut 16

The base block in this quilt uses a combination of teal/cream and pink/cream HSTs. The outer edge blocks use two HSTs of one color and a rectangle of the cream background, making an automatic cream border around the quilt top.

Use the Kaleidoscope Smart-Plate template to trim the pinwheels into 8-patch Kaleidoscope blocks, keeping the pink and teal fabrics in the corner wedge positions. (See page 14 for detailed cutting instructions.)

CUTTING ALTERNATE BLOCKS

Cut 25 squares 6½" x 6½" from the cream background fabric.

Fussy-cut 16 squares 6½" x 6½" of patterned fabric.

FRAMING THE FUSSY-CUT CENTERS

If the fussy-cut motifs are smaller than 6½", add a frame of background fabric strips to each square. I suggest a border of not less than 1"–1½" be added to each side. Then you can cut the block down to the size needed (in this case, 6½").

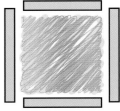

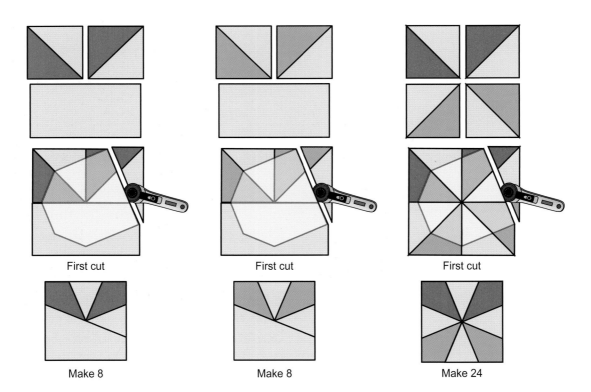

First cut

First cut

First cut

Make 8

Make 8

Make 24

PUTTING THE QUILT TOP TOGETHER

Follow the quilt top assembly diagram to arrange the blocks, being careful to create the circle effect around each of the fussy-cut blocks as shown.

Sew the blocks into rows, then sew the rows together.

BORDERS

Cut 6 strips 2½" wide from the pink inner border fabric. Piece them end-to-end to make one long strip.

From the long pink strip:
Cut 2 strips 54½" and sew them to opposite sides of the quilt top.

Cut 2 strips 58½" and sew them to the remaining sides of the quilt top.

Cut 2 strips 6½" x 58½" lengthwise (parallel to the selvages) from the teal floral border fabric and sew them to opposite sides of the quilt top.

Cut 2 strips 6½" x 70½" lengthwise (parallel to the selvages) from the teal floral border fabric and sew them to the remaining sides of the quilt top.

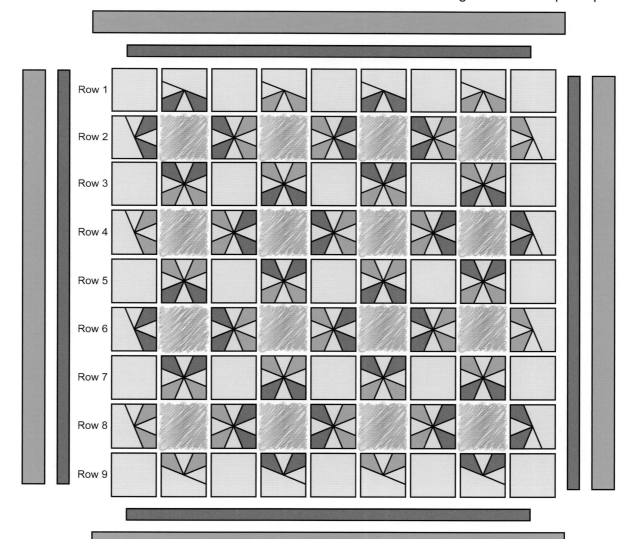

Row 1
Row 2
Row 3
Row 4
Row 5
Row 6
Row 7
Row 8
Row 9

Quilt top assembly

NORTHERN LIGHTS

42" x 42" finished size

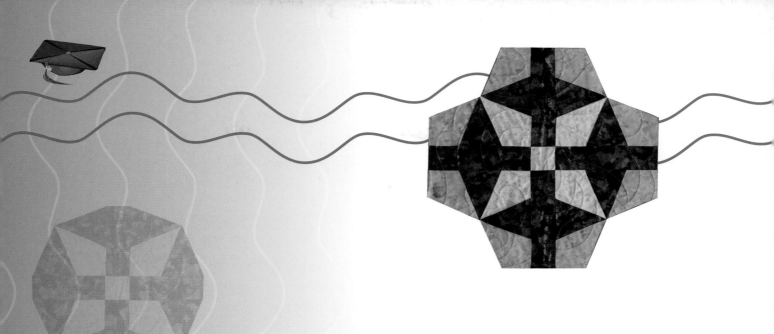

The Kaleidoscope block with a simple sashing and cornerstone frame gives the appearance of a four-pointed star.

This quilt is made with 6" finished 8-patch Kaleidoscope blocks.

MATERIALS

½ yard Light Blue

⅓ yard Green

½ yard Medium Blue

1⅛ yards Dark Blue background

¼ yard Light Blue inner border

¼ yard Medium Blue middle border

⅔ yard Green outer border

Backing to fit (approximately 3 yards)

Binding ⅜ yard

Batting 50" x 50"

MAKING THE PINWHEELS

Use half-square triangle method #2 or #3 (pages 9–11) to make the HST units.

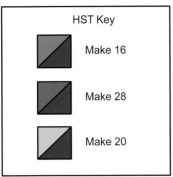

HST Key

Make 16

Make 28

Make 20

Follow the figures to arrange the HST combinations for the blocks.

Use the Kaleidoscope Smart-Plate template to trim the pinwheels into 8-patch Kaleidoscope blocks, keeping the lighter colored fabrics in the corner wedge positions. (See page 14 for detailed cutting instructions.)

SASHING AND CORNERSTONES

Cut 24 rectangles 2" x 6½" of dark blue
Cut 5 squares 2" x 2" of light blue
Cut 4 squares 2" x 2" of green

PUTTING THE QUILT TOP TOGETHER

Follow the quilt top assembly diagram (page 33) for placement and orientation of each of the blocks. Use a design wall to arrange the blocks properly for piecing the quilt top together.

Sew a sashing strip to the right side of the first 3 blocks of each row. (Do not sew a sashing strip to the fourth block in the row. The outer edges of the quilt top do not have sashing strips.) Sew the blocks together in rows.

Note the color placement of the cornerstones. Sew the 2" x 2" squares to sashing strips to form a sashing/cornerstone row.

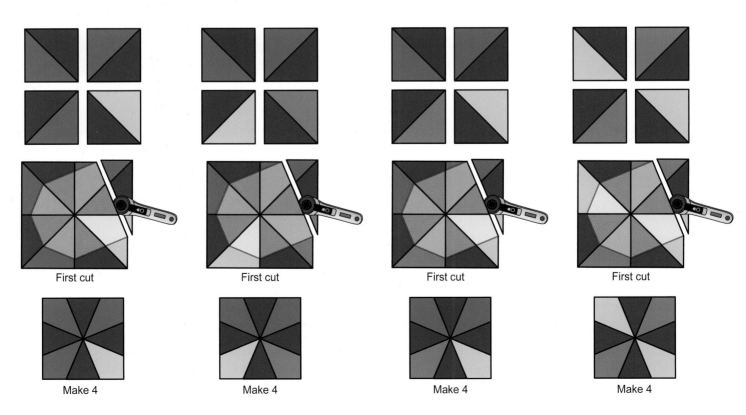

First cut

First cut

First cut

First cut

Make 4

Make 4

Make 4

Make 4

Sew the block and sashing/cornerstone rows together.

ADDING BORDERS

Cut 2 strips 2" x 29" of light blue and add to opposite sides of the quilt top. Cut 2 strips 2" x 32" and add to the remaining sides.

Cut 2 strips 1½" x 32" of medium blue and add to opposite sides of the quilt top. Cut 2 strips 1½" x 34" and add to the remaining sides.

Cut 2 strips 4½" x 34" of green and add to opposite sides of the quilt top. Cut 2 strips 4½" x 42" and add to the remaining sides.

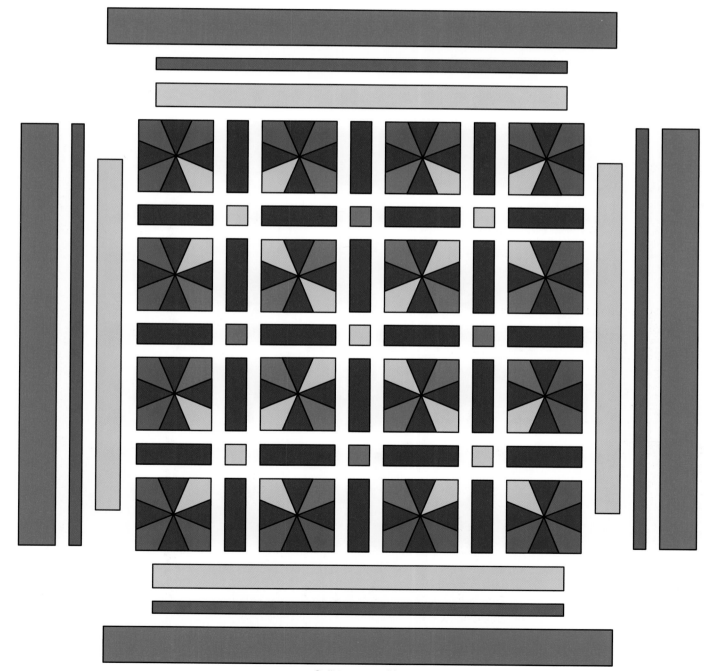

Quilt top assembly

STARS & STRIPES

94" x 94" finished size

There are only 25 blocks in this patriotic quilt. The simple blocks and large pieces help make this queen-size quilt come together quickly.

This quilt is made with 6" finished 8-patch Kaleidoscope blocks. With the addition of the star points, the unfinished blocks are 14½" x 14½".

MATERIALS

4⅝ yards White
3⅔ yards Blue
3 yards Red
Backing to fit (approximately 9 yards)
Binding ¾ yard
Batting 102" x 102"

MAKING THE PINWHEELS

Use half-square triangle method #2 or #3 (pages 9–11) to make the HST units.

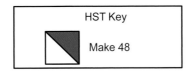

HST Key

Make 48

Follow the figures to make 12 Pinwheel blocks.

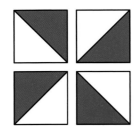

Use the Kaleidoscope Smart-Plate template to trim the pinwheels into 8-patch Kaleidoscope blocks, keeping the white fabric in the corner wedge positions. (See page 14 for detailed cutting instructions.)

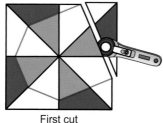

First cut

Make 12

MAKING THE STAR POINT BLOCKS

The star points are made by trimming quarter-square triangles (QST) into rectangles.

To make a quarter-square triangle unit, cut:
- 12 squares 7½" x 7½" of white
- 12 squares 7½" x 7½" of blue
- 24 squares 7½" x 7½" of red

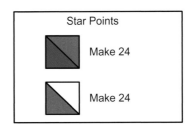

Star Points

Make 24

Make 24

Use half-square triangle method #1 (page 9) to make the star point HST units.

Align the seams of a red/white HST unit and a blue/red HST unit, right sides together, so that the red patches are opposite each other. Pin to keep the seams nested against each other.

Use method #1 of making HST units with the pair of HST units, sewing across the seams.

Cut apart to reveal 2 QST units

Trim the QST unit to make the star point (see figure on page 37).

Place the QST unit on your cutting surface with the white patch at the top. Place a square ruler on the patch so that the 6½" marking on the top edge of the ruler and the right edge of the ruler are both touching the diagonal seam (as noted with the yellow dots and black arrows in the illustration).

Trim away excess along the right side and top edge of the patch.

Rotate the QST unit so the blue patch is at the top.

Place a square ruler on the patch so that the 6½" marking on the top edge of the ruler is aligned with the edge of the patch just trimmed and the 4¾" marking on the right edge of the ruler is touching the diagonal seam.

Trim away excess along the right side and top edge of the patch. This will create an off-center trim resulting in a rectangle that measures 6½" x 4¾".

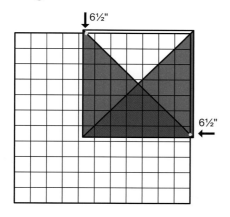

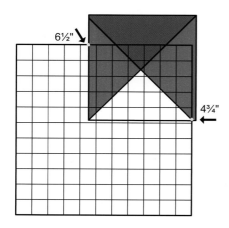

Make a total of 48 star point rectangles.

Cut 6 strips 4¾" wide from the white fabric and cut into 48 squares 4¾" x 4¾".

Assemble 12 Star blocks as shown.

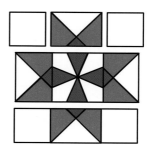

MAKING THE ALTERNATING BLOCK

From the white fabric, cut:
    3 strips 3½" wide
    8 strips 6½" wide

From the blue fabric, cut:
    3 strips 3½" wide
    8 strips 4¾" wide

Make 3 strip-sets with the 3½" wide strips as shown. Cut across the sets at 3½" to make a total of 26 patch sets. Sew the patch sets, alternating the colors, to make a total of (13) 4-patch units.

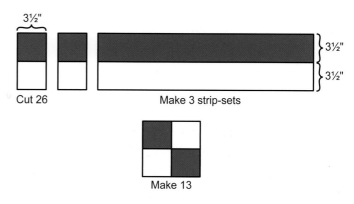

Make 4 strip-sets with 1 white 6½" wide strip and 2 blue 4¾" wide strips. Cut across the sets at 4¾" to make a total of 26 patch-sets.

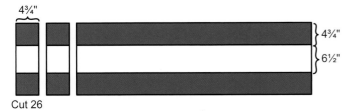

Cut 26

Cut the remaining 4 white strips at 4¾" to make a total of 26 white rectangles measuring 6½" x 4¾".

Assemble the alternating blocks as shown.

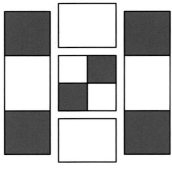

Make 13

Follow the quilt top assembly diagram for placement and orientation of each of the blocks.

BORDERS

The quilt top should measure 73" x 73" square.

Cut 9 strips of blue fabric 3½" wide and piece end-to-end as needed for the length of the border strips.

Cut 2 strips 3½" x 73" and add to opposite sides of the quilt top. Cut 2 strips 3½" x 79" and add to the remaining sides.

Cut 9 strips of white fabric 2½" wide and piece end-to-end.

Cut 2 strips 2½" x 79" and add to opposite sides of the quilt top. Cut 2 strips 2½" x 83" and add to the remaining sides.

Cut 11 strips of red fabric 6" wide and piece end-to-end.

Cut 2 strips 6" x 83" and add to opposite sides of the quilt top. Cut 2 strips 6" x 94" and add to the remaining sides.

Quilt top assembly

SEASCOPE

70" x 94" finished size

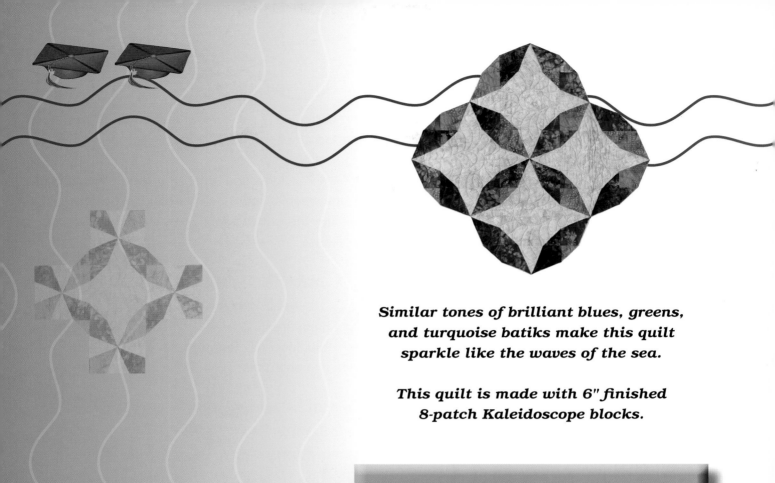

Similar tones of brilliant blues, greens, and turquoise batiks make this quilt sparkle like the waves of the sea.

This quilt is made with 6" finished 8-patch Kaleidoscope blocks.

MATERIALS

Choose four or more different batiks in a similar color range for this "2-color" quilt.
Total of 8 yards of Teal batiks
4⅔ yards of Beige batiks
1½ yards Teal batik for border & binding
Backing to fit (approximately 6 yards)
Batting 78" x 102"

Save the trimmings from the Pinwheel blocks to make a second funky and whimsical quilt or pillow.

Use silk pins to match the points. The fine pins will shift fabric less than thicker pins.

MAKING THE PINWHEELS

Use half-square triangle method #2 or #3 (pages 9–11) to make the HST units.

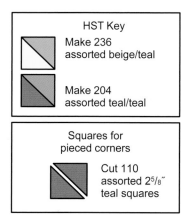

HST Key

Make 236
assorted beige/teal

Make 204
assorted teal/teal

Squares for pieced corners

Cut 110
assorted 2⅝″
teal squares

Use the HSTs randomly to make the various Pinwheel blocks to achieve the sparkling look. Note that some HSTs are all teal and some have from one to four segments of beige.

Use the Kaleidoscope Smart-Plate template to trim the pinwheels into 8-patch Kaleidoscope blocks, keeping the colored fabrics in the corner wedge positions.

MAKING THE ALTERNATE SNOWBALL BLOCKS

Cut 55 squares 6½" x 6½" of beige batik and use the Kaleidoscope Smart-Plate template to trim them into octagons.

Cut (110) 2⅝" squares of the various teal fabrics. Cut them in half on the diagonal for the corner pieces.

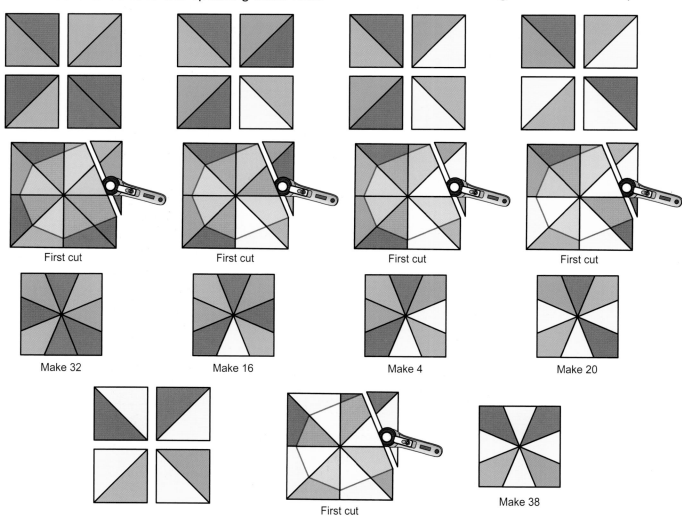

First cut

First cut

First cut

First cut

Make 32

Make 16

Make 4

Make 20

First cut

Make 38

Add 4 triangles to opposite sides of the octagons to make the Snowball blocks, randomly distributing the colors.

Make 55

PUTTING THE QUILT TOP TOGETHER

Follow the quilt top assembly diagram for placement and orientation of each of the blocks.

Sew the blocks into rows, then sew the rows together to create the quilt top.

BORDERS

Cut 10 strips of teal batik 2½" wide and piece end-to-end as needed for the length of the border strips.

Cut 2 strips 2½" x 66½" and add to the top and bottom of the quilt.

Cut 2 strips 2½" x 94½" long and add them to the sides.

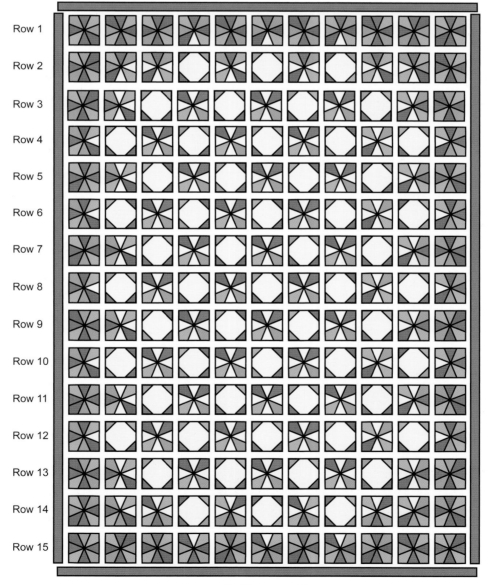

Row 1
Row 2
Row 3
Row 4
Row 5
Row 6
Row 7
Row 8
Row 9
Row 10
Row 11
Row 12
Row 13
Row 14
Row 15

Quilt top assembly

YES, A SCRAP QUILT!

28" x 28"; designed by Ellen Greenberg-Friedman, Teaneck, New Jersey;
made by the author

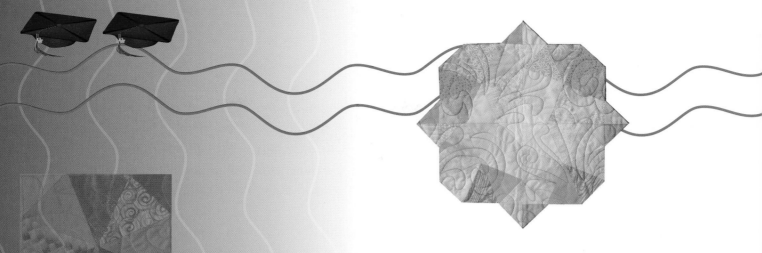

This contemporary Kaleidoscope quilt sparkles. It is so simple to make, using fabric scraps and only 4 different blocks.

This quilt is made with 6" finished 12-patch Kaleidoscope blocks.

MATERIALS

Assorted 4¼"–5" squares including:

6 golden yellow	22 violet
10 orange	10 blue
16 red	

Assorted 2⅝" squares including:

2 light yellow	4 violet
10 orange	10 blue
6 red	

Border ⅜ yard
Backing to fit (approximately 1 yard)
Binding ¼ yard
Batting 32" x 32"

The 6" finished 12-patch version of the Kaleidoscope block can start with a 7" unfinished Pinwheel block made up of 3¾" HST units.

MAKING THE PINWHEELS

Because the pieces are small and only used a couple of times each, the best choice is half-square triangle method #1 (page 9).

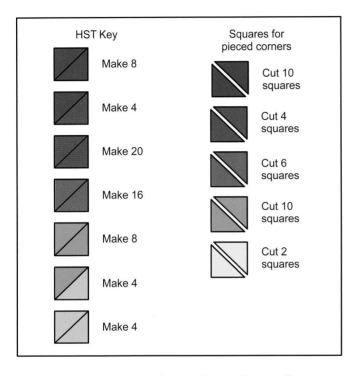

SHARON'S SHORTCUT

The HSTs of the same color represent different fabrics of the same color family. Make same-color HST units with two different fabrics of the same color to achieve the facet effect.

Follow the diagrams to arrange the half-square triangles for the 16 blocks used in this quilt.

Use the Kaleidoscope Smart-Plate template to trim the Pinwheel blocks into octagons for the 12-patch version of the Kaleidoscope block.

Cut 2⅝" x 2⅝" squares in half on the diagonal for the corner triangles and add to the octagons as shown to complete the Kaleidoscope blocks.

PUTTING THE QUILT TOP TOGETHER

Four different blocks make up one quadrant of the quilt top. The quadrants are all the same, they are simply rotated to create the design.

Follow the quadrant diagram for the placement of the blocks to make a quadrant. Repeat the process until all 4 quadrants are complete.

Arrange the quadrants as shown in the quilt top assembly diagram on page 47 and sew them together.

BORDERS

Cut 2 strips 2½" x 24½" of border fabric and add to opposite sides of the quilt top.

Cut 2 strips 2½" x 28½" of border fabric and add to the remaining sides of the quilt top.

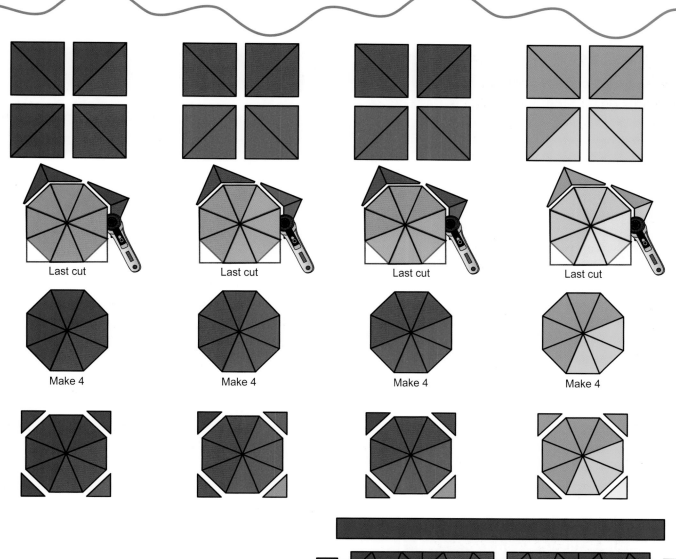

Last cut

Last cut

Last cut

Last cut

Make 4

Make 4

Make 4

Make 4

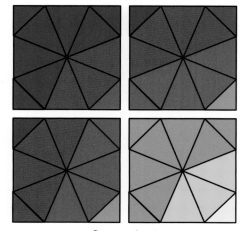

One quadrant
Make 4

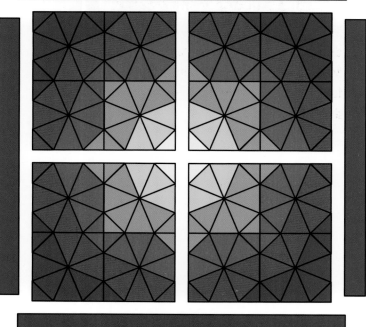

Quilt top assembly

OLD FASHION CHARM

36" x 48" finished size

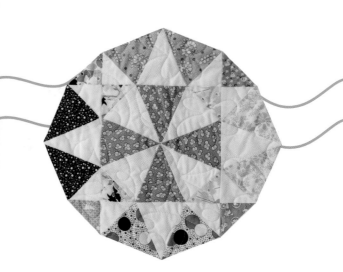

What could be more traditional than a '30s' style Kaleidoscope quilt made with '30s' style fabrics?

This quilt is made with 6" finished 12-patch Kaleidoscope blocks.

MATERIALS

2 packs 4¾"–5" assorted '30s' style "Charm Squares" of 35 different fabrics (or a total of 1⅓ yards)

2 squares 2⅝" x 2⅝" of each of 18 different fabrics (or a total of ½ yard)

2¼ White background and border

¾ yard Blue floral border and binding

Backing to fit (Approx. 1½ yards)

Batting 40" x 52"

Charm packs are a great way to make a scrappy-looking quilt.

MAKING THE PINWHEELS

Use half-square triangle method #1 (page 9) to make the HST units.

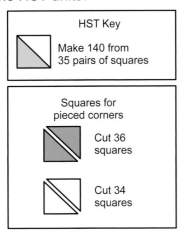

HST Key

Make 140 from 35 pairs of squares

Squares for pieced corners

Cut 36 squares

Cut 34 squares

Follow the diagrams to make the Pinwheel blocks.

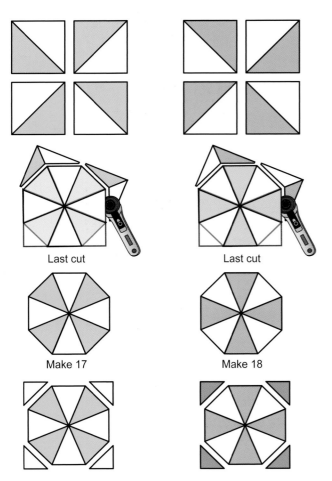

Last cut

Last cut

Make 17

Make 18

Use the Kaleidoscope Smart-Plate template to trim the pinwheels into octagons for the 12-patch Kaleidoscope blocks.

SHARON'S SHORTCUT

Arrange the octagons on a design surface to balance the colors. Then sew either white or colored corner triangles as needed for the alternate blocks.

Cut (36) 2⅝" x 2⅝" colored squares and (34) 2⅝" x 2⅝" white squares in half on the diagonal for the corner triangles. Add to the octagons to complete the Kaleidoscope blocks.

PUTTING THE QUILT TOP TOGETHER

The layout of blocks is random but be sure to alternate the blocks with white in the corners with the blocks that have color in the corners. Refer to the quilt top assembly diagram on page 51.

Sew blocks into 7 rows of 5 blocks each, then sew the rows together.

BORDERS

Cut 4 strips 1½" wide across the width of the white fabric.

Cut 4 strips 2½" wide across the width of the blue floral fabric.

Sew 4 white and blue floral strip-sets as the inner and outer borders will be sewn to the quilt top together as one border.

If the sets are not 42½" long, you may have to piece strips so they will be long enough for the sides.

Add the borders to the sides of the quilt.

Trim 2 strips-sets to the width of the quilt and sew to the top and bottom of the quilt top.

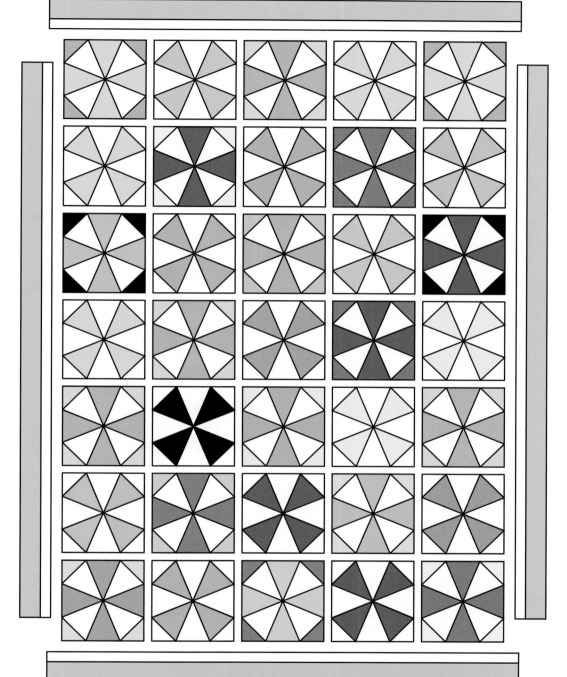

Quilt top assembly

The 6" finished 12-patch version of the Kaleidoscope block can start with an 8½" unfinished Pinwheel made of 4½" HST units or a 7" unfinished Pinwheel block made up of 3¾" HST units. Therefore, if your charm squares are a bit small, it is not going to adversely affect your blocks.

SQUARE IN A STAR

55" x 55" finished size

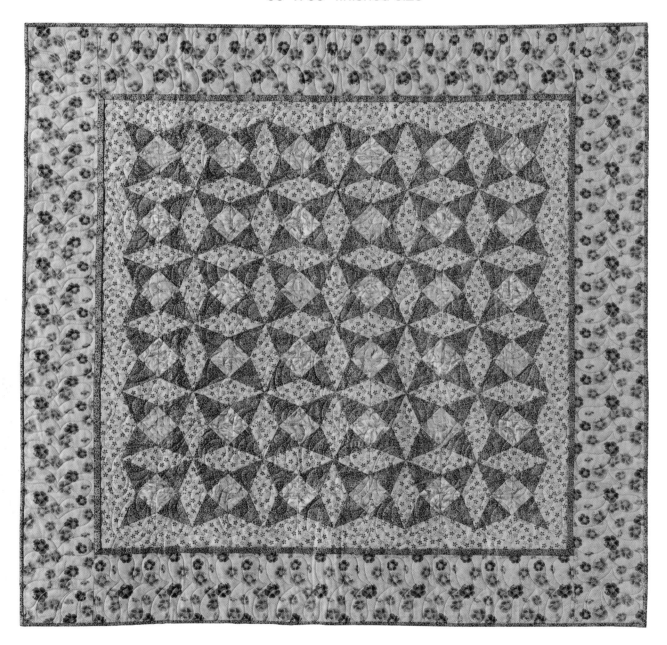

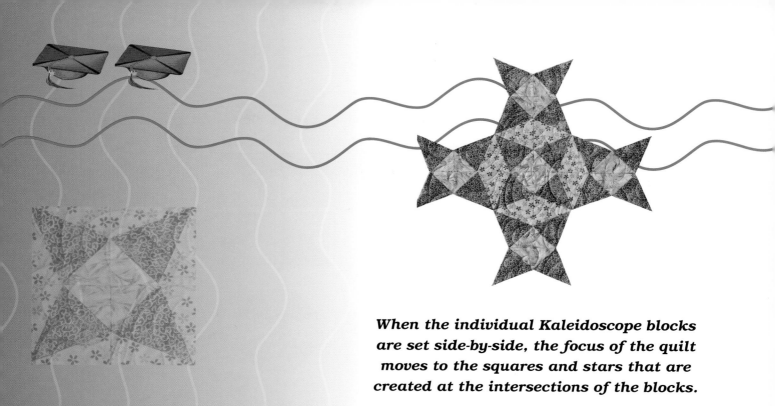

When the individual Kaleidoscope blocks are set side-by-side, the focus of the quilt moves to the squares and stars that are created at the intersections of the blocks.

This quilt is made with 6" finished 12-patch Kaleidoscope blocks.

MATERIALS

⅞ yard Dark Purple
⅓ yard Light Purple
⅞ yard Dark Green
⅓ yard Light Green
3 yards background
¼ yard inner border (Dark Purple)
1⅝ yard outer border
Binding ½ yard (Dark Purple)
Backing to fit (approximately 3¾ yards)
Batting 63" x 63"

The outer edge blocks that create the pieced border are simplified by using rectangles of the border fabric.

MAKING THE PINWHEELS

Use half-square triangle method #2 or #3 (pages 9–11) to make the HST units.

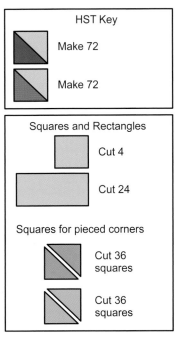

HST Key

Make 72

Make 72

Squares and Rectangles

Cut 4

Cut 24

Squares for pieced corners

Cut 36 squares

Cut 36 squares

All the Pinwheel blocks are the same. Follow the diagrams to arrange the half-square triangle combinations needed for the 25 Kaleidoscope blocks used in this quilt.

Use the Kaleidoscope Smart-Plate template to trim the pinwheels into octagons for the 12-patch Kaleidoscope blocks.

Cut 36 squares 2⅝" x 2⅝" each of light green and light purple in half on the diagonal for the corner tri-

SHARON'S SHORTCUT

The four corner blocks can be simplified even more with the use of faux triangles and rectangles. Replace each background square and HST combo with a rectangle and square of colored fabric.

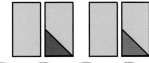

angles and add to the octagons as shown to complete the Kaleidoscope blocks.

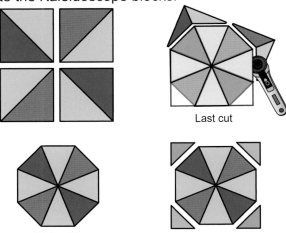

Last cut

Make 25

Arrange the remaining HST units and rectangles as shown on page 55 for the side and corner blocks. Trim them as for an 8-patch Kaleidoscope, then trim the corners indicated and add triangles to complete the blocks.

PUTTING THE QUILT TOP TOGETHER

Follow the quilt top assembly diagram (page 56) for placement and orientation of each of the blocks.

Sew the blocks into rows, then sew the rows together.

BORDERS

Trim ¾" from each of the 4 sides of the quilt top. See the Designer's Note on page 55. The trimmed top should measure 41" x 41".

Cut 4 strips 1½" wide of inner border fabric. Fold and press them lengthwise for a folded flange-style inner border (page 20).

Cut 2 strips 6½" x 41" lengthwise (parallel to the selvages) and sew to opposite sides of the quilt top, sandwiching in the folded inner border.

Cut 2 strips 6½" x 55" lengthwise and sew to the remaining sides of the quilt top, again sandwiching in the folded inner border.

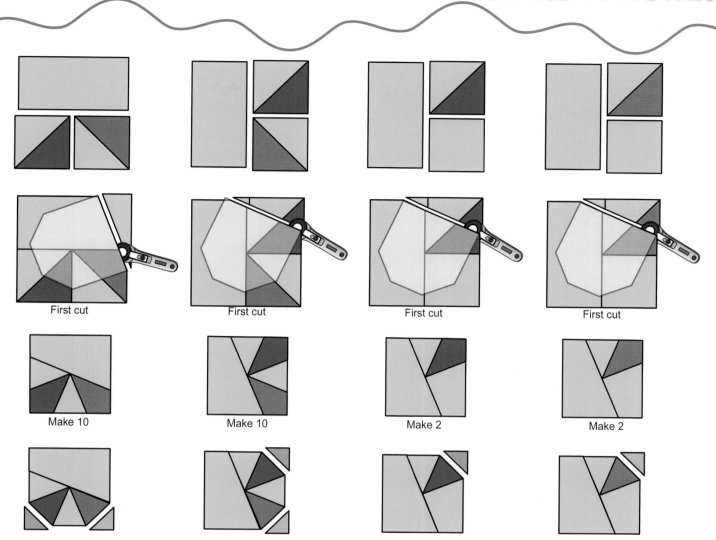

First cut

First cut

First cut

First cut

Make 10

Make 10

Make 2

Make 2

Designer's Note: The pieced border background would be too bold if left as a full 6" block. Therefore, ¾" is trimmed from the edges before the borders are added.

*Note: The (25) 12-patch Kaleidoscope blocks can start with a 7" Pinwheel block made up of 3¾" HST units. However, the outer border blocks should use the typical 8½" Pinwheel blocks made of 4½" HST unit for the 6" combination Kaleidoscope block.

Because there are so many points to match, try pinning each of the matching points ¼" from the raw edges through the seams with fine silk pins.

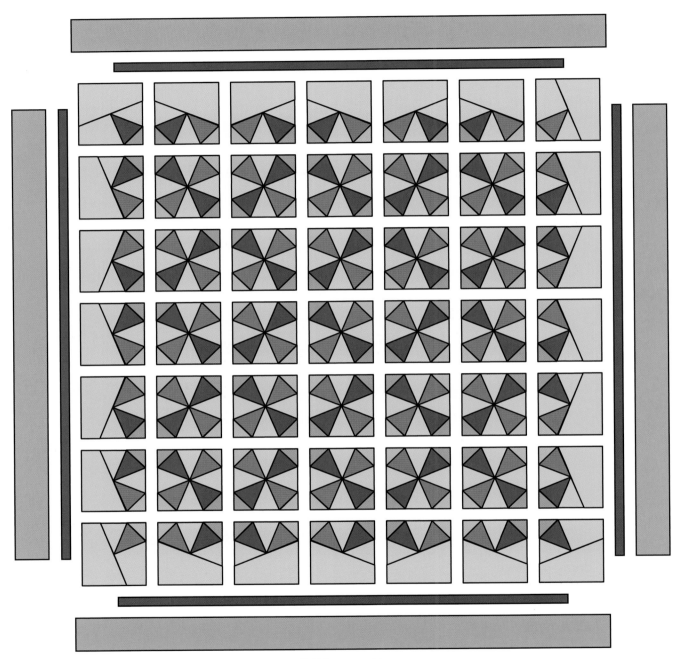

Quilt top assembly

SQUARE IN A STAR II, 55" x 55", was made by the author using the same pattern as SQUARE IN A STAR.

CLASSIC BLUE AND WHITE

42" x 54" finished size

Use the traditional arrangement of the two versions of the Kaleidoscope blocks in this timeless combination of blue and white.

This quilt is made with both the 6" finished 8-patch and 12-patch Kaleidoscope blocks.

MATERIALS

1 yard Light (White with blue accent)
⅞ yard Medium (White with dense blue print)
2 yards of Dark (Blue with white accent)
1⅝ yards of large print border fabric
Backing to fit (approximately 3 yards)
Binding ⅜ yard
Batting 50" x 62"

The 12-patch Kaleidoscope blocks can start with a 7" Pinwheel block made up of 3¾" HST units. However, the 8-patch blocks and combination blocks should use the 8½" Pinwheel blocks made of 4½" HSTs.

MAKING THE PINWHEELS

A combination of the various methods may be the most efficient way to make the variety of HST units needed for this quilt (pages 9–11).

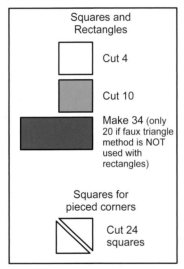

HST Key

Make 34 (+4 if faux triangles method is NOT used with rectangles)

Make 10

Make 28 (+10 if faux triangles method is NOT used with rectangles)

Squares and Rectangles

Cut 4

Cut 10

Make 34 (only 20 if faux triangle method is NOT used with rectangles)

Squares for pieced corners

Cut 24 squares

Follow the Pinwheel diagram to arrange the half-square triangle combination for (8) 8-patch Kaleidoscope blocks. Trim as shown.

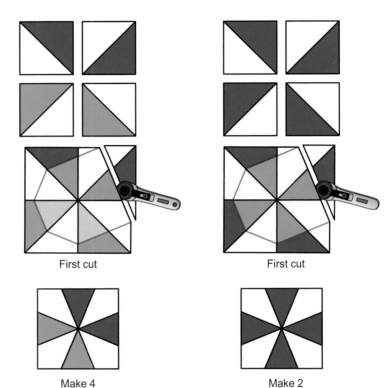

First cut   First cut

Make 4   Make 2

Follow the Pinwheel diagrams to arrange the half-square triangle combinations needed for the (7) 12-Patch Kaleidoscope blocks. Trim as shown.

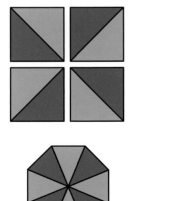

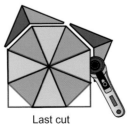

Last cut

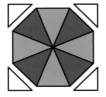

Make 7

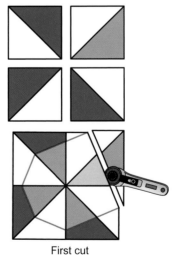

First cut

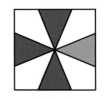

Make 2

Note the placement of the various kite-shaped corner wedges in the 8-patch blocks to be sure that you trim the blocks correctly.

Use the squares and rectangles to make the 20 combination blocks. Use the Kaleidoscope Smart-Plate template to trim them as shown.

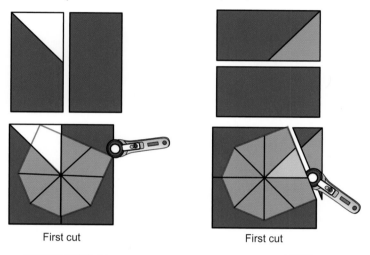

First cut

First cut

Make 4

Make 10

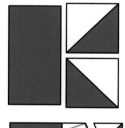

First cut

Make 6

Trim 2 corners from the 10 combination blocks indicated.

Cut 2⅝" x 2⅝" squares in half on the diagonal for the corner triangles and add to the octagons and combination blocks as shown to complete the Kaleidoscope blocks.

Follow the quilt top assembly diagram (page 62) for placement and orientation of each of the blocks. Arrange in 7 rows of 5 blocks each.

Sew the blocks into rows, then sew the rows together.

BORDERS

Cut the border fabric for long border strips that do not need to be pieced. Use the remaining fabric for binding strips.

Cut 2 strips 6½" x 42½" lengthwise (parallel to the selvages) and sew to the sides of the quilt.

Cut 2 strips 6½" x 30½" lengthwise (parallel to the selvages) and sew to the top and bottom of the quilt.

Quilt top assembly

Alternate color ideas

WEB OF TROUBLE

45" x 45" finished size

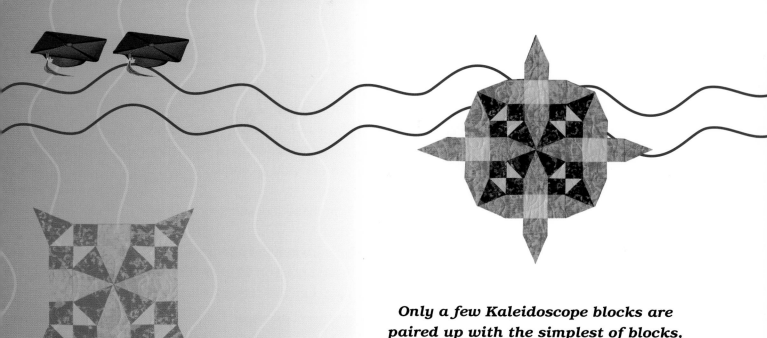

Only a few Kaleidoscope blocks are paired up with the simplest of blocks, a modified Nine-Patch, to create this complex looking design.

This quilt is made with both 6" finished 8-patch and 12-patch Kaleidoscope blocks.

MATERIALS

2⅓ yards Dark Purple for blocks, border, and binding
1¼ yards Orange
1 yard Yellow
Backing to fit (approximately 3 yards)
Batting 53" x 53"

The alternate blocks are strip-pieced Nine-Patch blocks. The pieced border comes together super quick using the strip-piecing method, too.

MAKING THE PINWHEELS

You can use any of the techniques to make HST patches. Although one of the multiple HST unit methods may be a bit quicker, you could end up with extra HSTs.

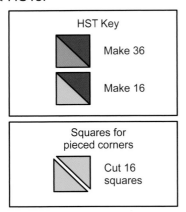

Follow the figures to make the Pinwheel blocks.

Trim these blocks as for a 12-patch block

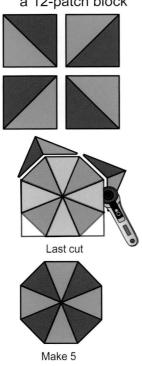

Last cut

Make 5

Cut 16 squares 2⅝" x 2⅝" from two 2⅝" wide strips of yellow fabric. Cut the squares on the diagonal to make the 32 triangles for the pieced Kaleidoscope corners. Add as shown.

Trim these blocks as for an 8-patch block.

Be sure that the appropriate fabric is in the corner wedge position when trimming the 8-patch blocks. Then trim the corners as indicated.

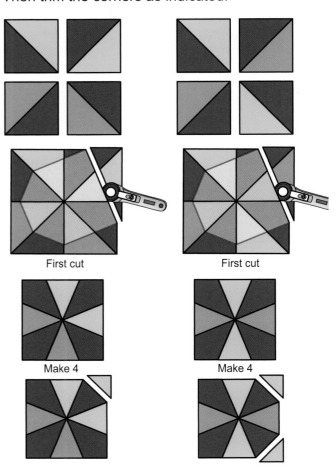

First cut　　　　First cut

Make 4　　　　Make 4

There is a variety of fabric combinations used in the Nine-Patch blocks and border pieces. Follow the strip-piecing instructions to make the appropriate number of patch-sets needed for the blocks and border. Some are used in more than one block or border piece, so I suggest you cut the pieces needed and keep them in piles of patch-sets.

As you make each block, take from the piles you need for the blocks. To have a visual of which patch-sets make up which blocks, you can lay out the patch sets and blocks on a design wall if you have one.

From the yellow fabric cut:
2 strips 2¼" wide
2 strips 4¾" wide
1 strip 3" wide, cut in half
    to make 2 strips 20" long.

From the purple fabric cut:
1 strip 3" wide
9 strips 2¼" wide strips; cut one in half
    to make 2 strips 20" long.

From the orange fabric cut:
4 strips 3" wide
3 strips 2¼" wide; cut one in half
    to make 2 strips 20" long.

Make the strip-sets and cut the patch-sets as indicated.

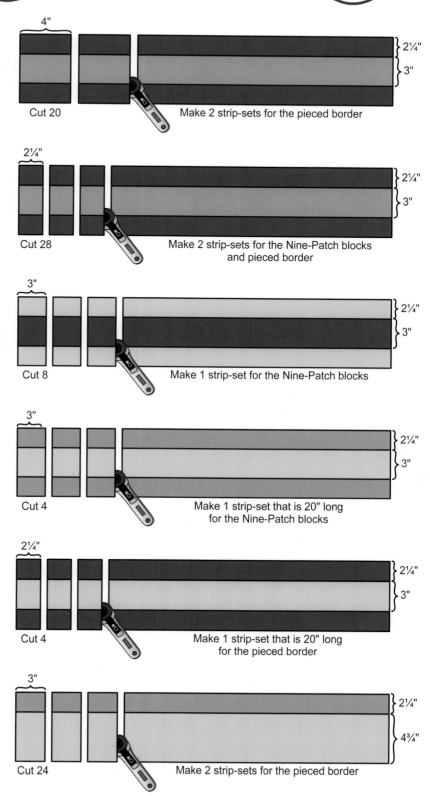

4"
Cut 20   Make 2 strip-sets for the pieced border   2¼" 3"

2¼"
Cut 28   Make 2 strip-sets for the Nine-Patch blocks and pieced border   2¼" 3"

3"
Cut 8   Make 1 strip-set for the Nine-Patch blocks   2¼" 3"

3"
Cut 4   Make 1 strip-set that is 20" long for the Nine-Patch blocks   2¼" 3"

2¼"
Cut 4   Make 1 strip-set that is 20" long for the pieced border   2¼" 3"

3"
Cut 24   Make 2 strip-sets for the pieced border   2¼" 4¾"

Make the 12 Nine-Patch blocks as shown.

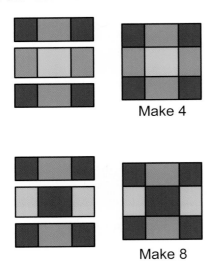

Make 4

Make 8

Follow the quilt top assembly diagram (page 69) for placement and orientation of each of the blocks, alternating the Kaleidoscope and Nine-Patch blocks in 5 rows of 5 blocks each.

Sew the blocks into rows, then sew the rows together.

BORDERS

Join the patch-sets for the top and bottom borders as shown in the quilt top diagram and add to the quilt top.

Join the patch-sets for the side borders and add to the quilt top.

Cut 6 strips of dark purple fabric 2¼" wide and sew end-to-end as needed for the length of the border strips.

Cut 2 strips 2¼" x 42" and add to the sides of the quilt.

Cut 2 strips 2¼" x 46" and add to the remaining sides.

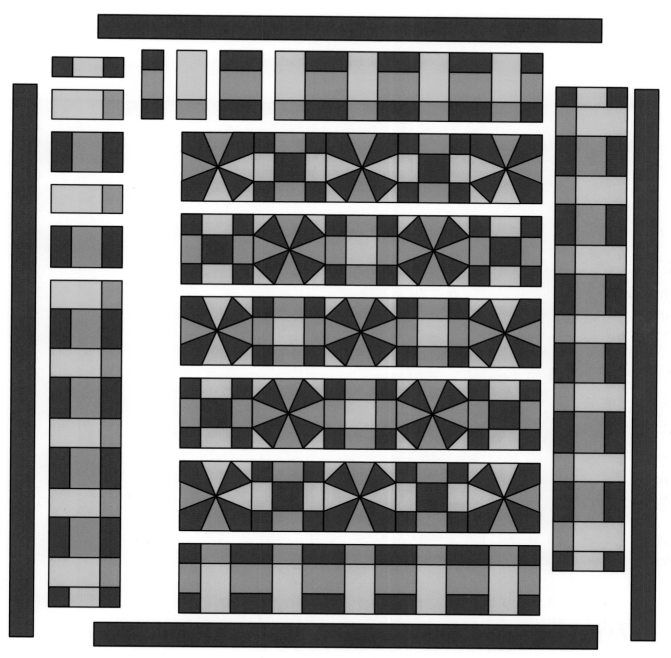

Quilt top assembly

APPLE BLOSSOM

57" x 57" finished size

*Choice of fabrics and fabric placement
would change the look of this classic
use of Kaleidoscope blocks.*

*This quilt is made with both 6" finished
8-patch and 12-patch Kaleidoscope blocks.*

MATERIALS

1⅝ yards Dark Red (includes inner border)

⅝ yard Dark Green

1⅝ yards Deep Pink

1¼ yards Light Green

⅞ yard Beige with overall small print of apple blossoms

2¾ yard Beige with overall medium to large print of blossoms and apples (includes fabric for blocks and lengthwise cuts for unpieced border strips)

Backing to fit (approximately 3⅞ yards)

Binding ½ yard (Dark Red)

Batting 65" x 65"

*The 12-patch Kaleidoscope blocks can start
with a 7" Pinwheel block made up of 3¾" HST
units. However, the (12) 8-patch and 24 outer
border blocks should use the typical 8½"
Pinwheel blocks with 4½" HST units.*

MAKING THE PINWHEELS

Use half-square triangle method #2 or #3 (pages 9–11) to make the HST units.

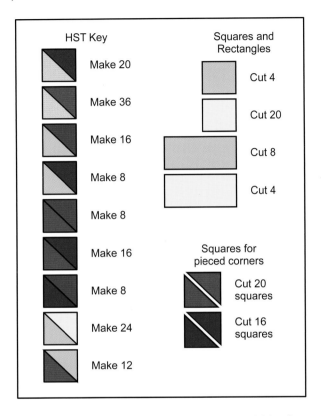

Follow the diagrams to make the Pinwheel blocks for (13) 12-patch Kaleidoscope blocks. Use the Kaleidoscope Smart-Plate template to trim them.

Follow the diagrams on page 73 to make the Pinwheel blocks for the (12) 8-patch Kaleidoscope blocks. Use the Kaleidoscope Smart-Plate template to trim them, being careful to place the correct colors in the corner wedge positions.

Follow the diagrams on page 74 to make the outer blocks. Using rectangles eliminates some of the piec-ing. They form an automatic pieced border around the design. Use the Kaleidoscope Smart-Plate template to trim them.

Cut 2 strips each dark red and deep pink fabrics 2⅝" wide. Cut 16 dark red and 20 deep pink 2⅝" x 2⅝" squares.

Cut the squares in half on the diagonal for the corner triangles and add them as shown to complete the 12-patch and outer blocks.

Follow the quilt top assembly diagram (page 75) for placement and orientation of each of the blocks.

Sew the blocks into rows, then sew the rows together.

BORDERS

The inner border is narrow and in a contrasting fabric and the outer border is the same fabric used in the outer blocks. This combination creates a "floating frame" effect.

Cut 5 strips 2" wide of dark red and sew end-to-end as needed for the length of the inner border strips.

Cut 2 inner border strips 2" x 42½" and add to opposite sides of the quilt top.

Cut 2 inner border strips 2" x 45½" and add to remaining sides of the quilt top.

Cut 2 outer border strips lengthwise 6½" x 45½" and add to opposite sides of the quilt top.

Cut 2 outer border strips lengthwise 6½" x 57½" and add to remaining sides of the quilt top.

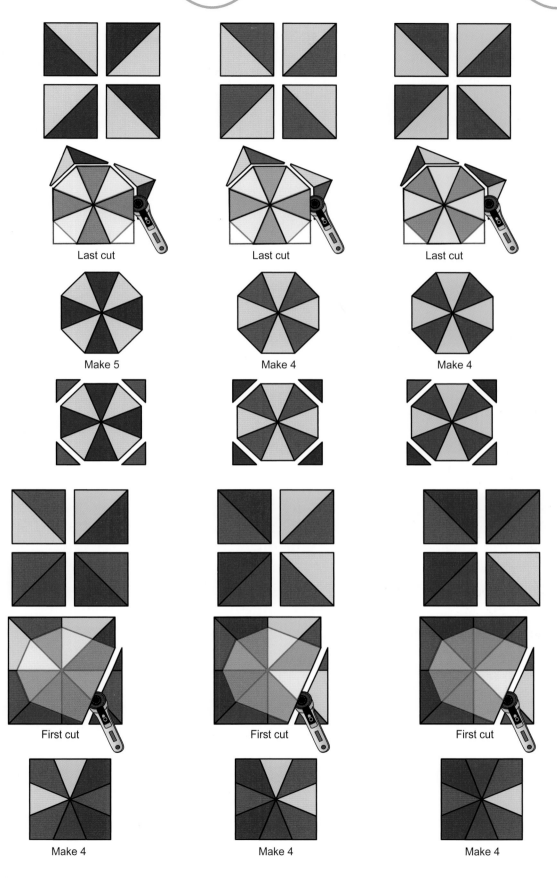

Last cut

Last cut

Last cut

Make 5

Make 4

Make 4

First cut

First cut

First cut

Make 4

Make 4

Make 4

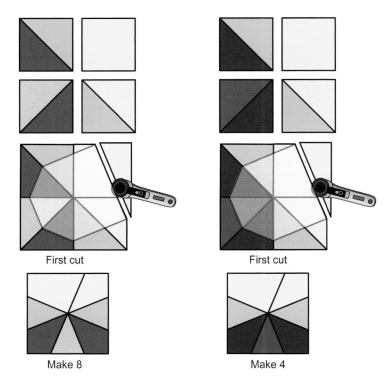

First cut   First cut

Make 8   Make 4

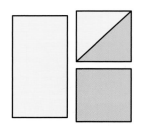
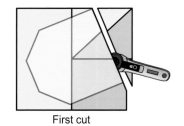
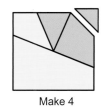

First cut

Make 4   Make 4

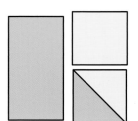
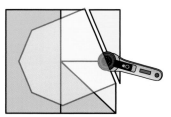
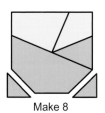

First cut

Make 8   Make 4   Make 4

Quilt top assembly

75

ENGLISH GARDEN

58" x 70" finished size

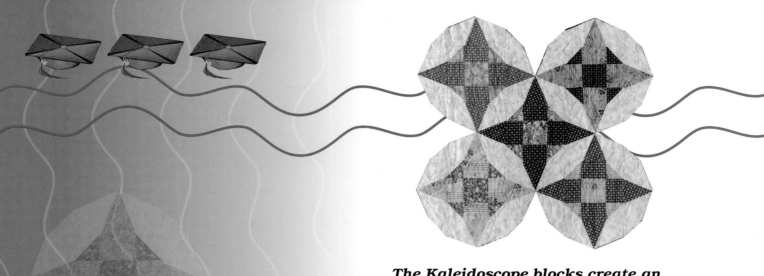

The Kaleidoscope blocks create an illusion of curves in this fat quarter-friendly design.

This quilt is made with 6" finished 8-patch Kaleidoscope blocks.

MATERIALS

8 dark fat quarters
8 light fat quarters
3 yards Cream background
2 yards large print (for the pieced border)
Binding ⅝ yard Floral Blue
Backing fabric to fit (approximately 4½ yards)
Batting 66" x 78"

Use the fat-quarter cutting map (page 78) to ensure you can cut all you need from each fat quarter to complete the blocks.

Use extra fat quarters to make additional combinations for a scrappier look.

From each fat quarter cut:

1 square 9¾" x 9¾" for the Kaleidoscope
      pinwheel HST units

1 square 6¼" x 6¼" for the Churn Dash HST units

2 squares 3" x 3" for the Churn Dash centers

8 rectangles 3" x 2¼" for the Churn Dash
      side centers

Fat-quarter cutting map

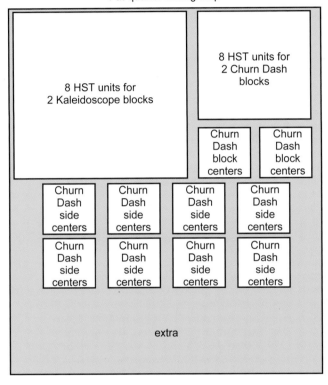

From the cream fabric cut:

21 or more squares 9¾" x 9¾"

16 or more squares 6¼" x 6¼"

2 strips 2⅝" wide for 16 squares 2⅝" x 2⅝" cut
      in half on the diagonal for block corners in the
      floral border

8 strips 2½" wide for the outer border

From the floral border print cut:

5 squares 9¾" x 9¾"

18 squares 6½" x 6½"

18 rectangles 4½" x 8½"

MAKING THE BLOCKS

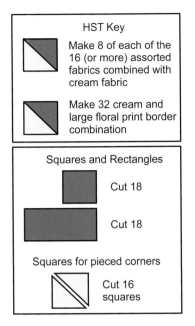

Use method #2 (pages 9–10) to make the HST units for both the Kaleidoscope and Churn Dash blocks.

Use the 9¾" squares for the Kaleidoscope pinwheel HSTs and the smaller 6¼" squares for the Churn Dash block HSTs.

If you would prefer to use method #1 (page 9), cut the squares in quarters and use the resulting, smaller 4⅞" and 3⅛" squares to make the HST units.

MAKING THE CHURN DASH BLOCKS

From the 16 (or more) fat quarters, choose light and dark fabric combinations for sets of blocks. Each combination will make 4 blocks—2 with dark centers and corners and 2 with light centers and corners.

Follow the block diagram to sew the small HST units, rectangles, and 3" squares in rows and the rows into the first set of 2 blocks. Reverse the dark and light fabrics to make the second set of 2 blocks.

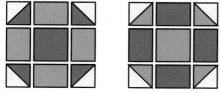

Make a total of 32

MAKING THE KALEIDOSCOPE BLOCKS

For the proper placement of fabrics, lay out the Churn Dash blocks on a design wall or other such surface to arrange them in a pleasing manner (see below). Leave space between each of the Churn Dash blocks for the Kaleidoscope blocks as they are prepared.

Match the fabric in a Kaleidoscope pinwheel HST with the side center rectangle on each Churn Dash block. Think of the locations of the Churn Dash blocks like the numbers on a clock—12 o'clock, 3 o'clock, 6 o'clock, and 9 o'clock. Then lay out the HST units in this order for each Pinwheel block.

Use the floral/cream HST units around the outside edges of your layout. (Refer to the quilt top assembly diagram, page 81.)

Join the HST units for the Pinwheel blocks. Use the Kaleidoscope Smart-Plate template to trim the Pinwheels to make (31) 8-patch Kaleidoscope blocks, keeping the cream fabric in the kite-shaped corner wedge positions.

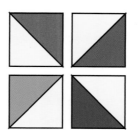
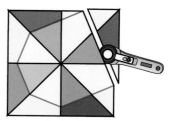

First cut

Make 31

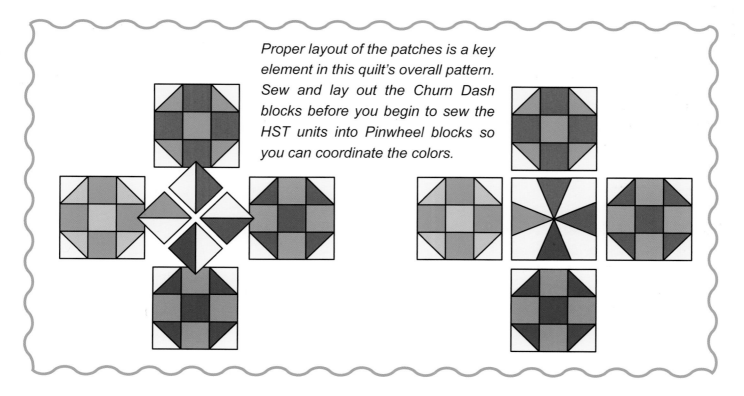

Proper layout of the patches is a key element in this quilt's overall pattern. Sew and lay out the Churn Dash blocks before you begin to sew the HST units into Pinwheel blocks so you can coordinate the colors.

PIECED BORDER BLOCKS

The pieced border closes the outer rings of cream with three different blocks.

Make the 18 border blocks with a floral border 4½" x 8½" rectangle and 2 HST units, one a floral border/ cream combination and the other a fat quarter/cream combination that matches the adjacent Churn Dash block (see the quilt top assembly diagram, page 81).

Sew the HST units together and complete the partial Pinwheel block with the rectangle.

Use the Kaleidoscope Smart-Plate template to trim, keeping the cream in the kite-shaped corner wedge position.

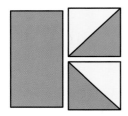 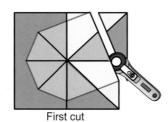

First cut

Make 18

Make 14 side blocks by adding 2 cream corner triangles to adjacent corners of a floral border 6½" square. Use the Kaleidoscope Smart-Plate template to cut 2 adjacent corners from the square of fabric. Then add 2 cream triangles to complete the block.

Make 14

Make 4 corner blocks by using the Kaleidoscope Smart-Plate template to cut one corner from (4) 6½" x 6½" squares of floral border fabric. Add a cream triangle to complete the blocks.

Make 4

BORDERS

Cut 8 strips 2½" wide of cream for outer borders. Sew the strips end-to-end as needed for the length of the border strips.

Cut 2 strips 2½" x 66½" long and attach to the sides of the quilt top.

Cut 2 strips 2½" 58½" long and attach to the top and bottom of the quilt top.

Bind with the blue floral fabric.

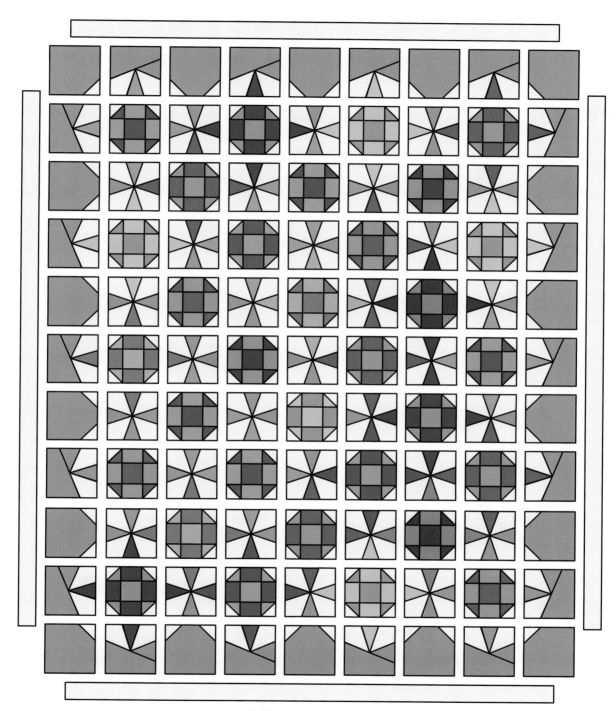

Quilt top assembly

PINK LEMONADE

74" x 74" finished size

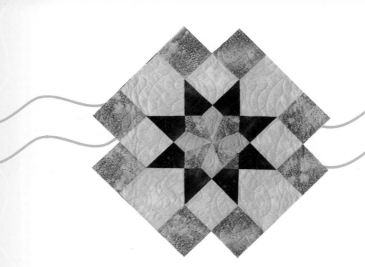

An "easier than it looks" Kaleidoscope Star is set on point, adding excitement and interest to the quilt.

The 14½" x 14½" blocks in this quilt are made with the 6" finished 8-patch Kaleidoscope block.

MATERIALS

2 yards Light Pink
1⅞ yards Medium Pink
2⅜ yards Dark Pink
2⅝ yards Yellow
Backing to fit (approximately 4⅞ yards)
Batting 82" x 82"
Binding ¾ yard

The quarter-square triangle (QST) method used for the star points is just as easy as making the HST units.

The only challenge here is setting the blocks on point. Don't let this scare you away. After seeing how easy it is, you may get hooked!

PINK LEMONADE

MAKING THE PINWHEELS FOR THE KALEIDOSCOPE BLOCKS

Use half-square triangle method #2 or #3 (pages 9–11) to make the HST units.

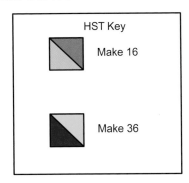

HST Key

Make 16

Make 36

Use the Kaleidoscope Smart-Plate template to trim the Pinwheel blocks, keeping the light pink in the corner wedge positions on the light pink/medium pink pinwheels and the dark pink in the corner wedge positions on the dark pink/yellow pinwheels as shown.

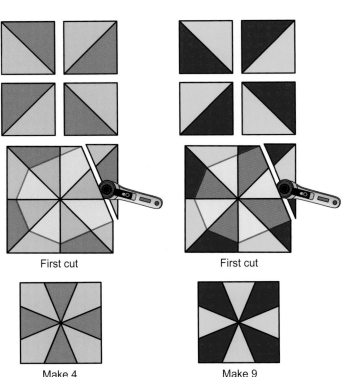

First cut   First cut

Make 4   Make 9

MAKING THE ALTERNATING BLOCKS

Cut 8 yellow strips 6½" wide
Cut 10 medium pink strips 4¾" wide

Make 5 strip-sets as shown. Cut 36 patch-sets 4¾" wide.

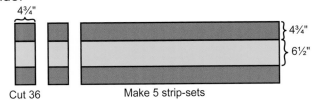

4¾"

4¾"
6½"

Cut 36   Make 5 strip-sets

Cut 18 rectangles 4¾" x 6½" from the remaining 3 yellow strips.

Assemble the alternating blocks as shown.

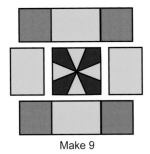

Make 9

MAKING THE STAR POINT BLOCKS

Star points are made by trimming a quarter-square triangle (QST) unit into a rectangular star point unit.

To make the QST units, cut:
4 squares 7½" x 7½" of medium pink
4 squares 7½" x 7½" of yellow
8 squares 7½" x 7½" of dark pink

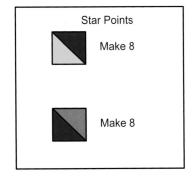

Star Points

Make 8

Make 8

Kaleidoscope the Smart Way   84   Sharon Sebrow

Use half-square triangle method #1 (page 9) to make 8 dark pink/yellow HST units and 8 dark pink/medium pink HST units.

Align the seams of 2 different HST units, right sides together, such that the dark pink patches are opposite each other. Pin to keep the seams tight up against each other.

Use the same method #1 of making HST units with the pair of HST units, sewing across the seams. Cut apart to reveal 2 quarter-square triangle units.

Trim the QST unit to make the rectangular star point section.

Place the QST unit on your cutting surface with the yellow patch at the top. Place a square ruler such that the 6½" marking on the top edge and the right edge of the ruler are both touching the diagonal seam (as noted with the yellow dots and black arrows in the illustration). Trim away excess along the right side and top of the patch.

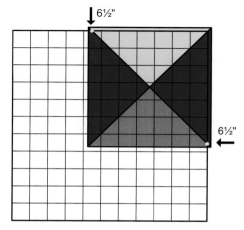

Rotate the QST unit so the medium pink patch is at the top. Place a square ruler such that the 6½"

marking on the top edge of the ruler is aligned with the edge of the patch just trimmed and the 4¾" marking on the right edge of the ruler is touching the diagonal seam. Trim away excess along the right side and top of the patch. This will create an off-center trim resulting in a rectangle that measures 6½" x 4¾".

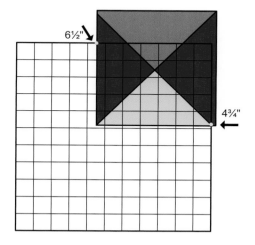

Make 16 star point rectangles.

PUTTING THE STAR BLOCK TOGETHER

Cut 2 yellow 4¾" wide strips into 16 squares 4¾" x 4¾".

Join the squares, star point units, and Kaleidoscope blocks as shown, matching the medium pink patches in the Kaleidoscope blocks and star point units.

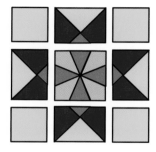

Arrange the blocks in diagonal rows for the on-point setting. Prepare the setting triangles and sew to the

ends of the rows before sewing the rows together. (See the quilt assembly diagram on page 87.)

SETTING TRIANGLES

The cutting measurements are slightly oversized. Trimming will be necessary.

Cut 2 light pink squares 17½" x 17½" twice on the diagonal for a total of 8 side setting triangles.

Cut 2 light pink squares 9½" x 9½" once on the diagonal to make a total of 4 corner setting triangles.

Cut 1 dark pink strip 15½" wide into 20 strips 2" x 15½".

Add 2 strips to the short sides of the 8 side setting triangles as shown.

Center and sew a 2" strip to the long side of the 4 corner setting triangles.

Trim the strips even with the sides of the triangles.

Join the triangles to the block rows as shown in the quilt top assembly diagram.

Once the triangles and rows are sewn in place, use a long ruler to measure ¼" from the intersecting points along the edges and trim away any excess fabric.

BORDERS

Measure your quilt top for borders. The quilt should be approximately 62" x 62".

Cut 16 dark pink strips 2" wide.

> Sew 7 of them end-to-end to create a long strip 2" wide.
>
> Repeat with 7 more strips to make a second long strip.
>
> Cut 8 pieces 2" x 6½" from the remaining strips. Set aside for cornerstones.

Cut 8 light pink strips 3½" wide.

> Sew 7 of them end-to-end to create a long strip 3½" wide.
>
> Make a strip-set of the long dark pink and light pink strips as shown below.
>
> Cut 4 segments 62" long or the measurement of your quilt top (border strip-set).
>
> Cut 4 segments 3½" x 3½".

Sew a 2" x 6½" dark pink strip to opposite sides of the 3½" strip-set segments to make 4 cornerstones.

Sew a border strip-set to the top and bottom of the quilt top.

Sew a cornerstone to both ends of the remaining 2 border strip-sets and add them to the remaining sides of the quilt top.

Quilt top assembly

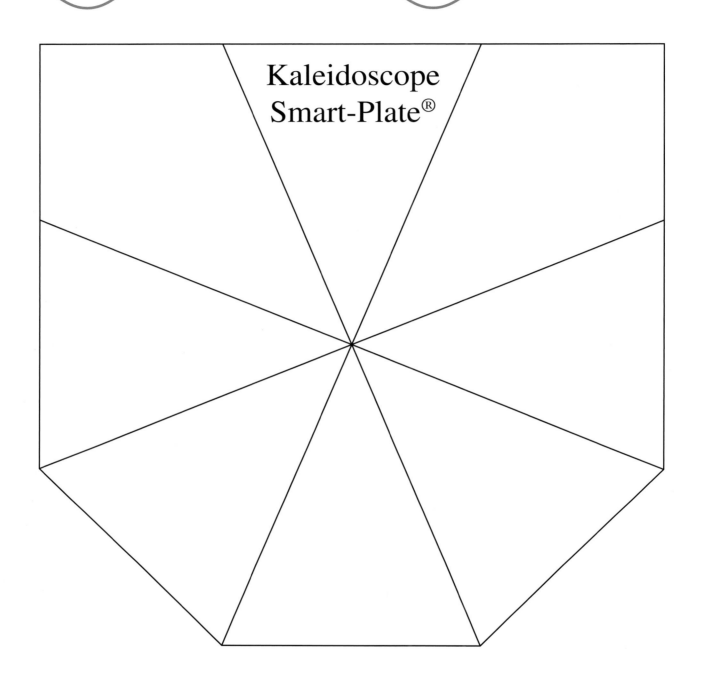

Kaleidoscope
Smart-Plate®

HOT TAMALE, 40" x 40", was made by the author using the same pattern as NORTHERN LIGHTS with a slight variation in the border.

RESOURCES

Thank you to the various companies of tools, fabric, and services who have offered their support in the completion of this book.

Action Studios
www.action-studios.com

Baby Lock USA
www.babylock.com

Blank Quilting
2 Bridge St. Suite 220
Irvington, NY 10533
Phone: 914-478-7900
Toll Free: 888-442-5265
Web site: www.blankquilting.com

Janice Jamison
415 Wallingford Terr.
Union, NJ 07083
908-686-0875
jjam061454@ad.com

Northcott Silk
640 Rowntree Dairy Road
Woodbridge, ON, L4L 5T8
Canada
Phone: (905) 850-6675
E-mail: info@northcott.net
Web site: www.northcott.net

P & B Textiles
1580 Gilbreth Road
Burlingame, CA 94010
Phone: 650-692-0422
Web site: www.pbtex.com

Red Rooster Fabrics
Wholesale only
Web site: www.redroosterfabrics.com

Ricky Tims Art Quilt Studio and Gallery
PO Box 392
105 W. Ryus Ave
La Veta, CO 81055
Phone: 719-742-3755
Web site: www.rickytims.com

For information on purchasing the Kaleidoscope Smart-Plate® templates, contact AQS or the author at www.smartplatequilting.com.

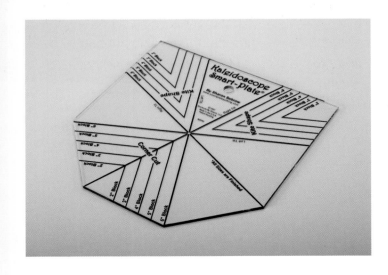

ABOUT THE AUTHOR

From a very young age, Sharon Sebrow has enjoyed hand needlework of all kinds. In high school home ec, Sharon had her first taste of machine sewing. It wasn't until she was pregnant with her first child, in 1989, that she started to do patchwork by machine. She fell in love with the immediate gratification the strip-piecing method provided. Once she started quilting, she took off and never looked back.

Every chance she could, Sharon would share her sewing and quilting knowledge. Whether it was teaching privately, as a guest quilter in kindergarten classes in her children's elementary school, in after-school clubs for second and third graders, or in the local community adult education program, Sharon found delight and fulfillment in teaching others how to sew and quilt.

Sharon Sebrow

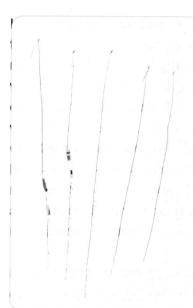

seeing the satisfac-
they are successful
chnique they thought
and discovering how
f her young students
4 New Jersey State
place and the other,
r, with an honorable
n when she had won
quilt the year before

estions and answers
Quilt Magazine. In addition to her column, Sharon began designing

quilts and writing patterns for the same publication. By the end of 2004, Sharon became features editor, reviewing new books and interviewing authors. At the end of 2005, Sharon took a break from to enjoy the final weeks of her pregnancy and perfect her design and technique for the Kaleidoscope Smart-Plate® template.

When the Cozy Quilt Shoppe in River Edge, New Jersey, opened just two miles from home, Sharon quickly became a permanent fixture and resident teacher there.

Sharon lives in northern New Jersey with her husband of 20 years, her five children, ranging in ages from 3 to 19, and their dog.